The Appalachian
Indian Frontier

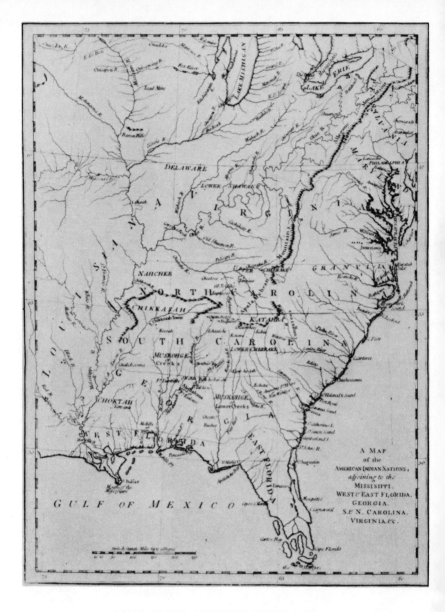

A MAP OF THE AMERICAN INDIAN NATIONS

From James Adair, *History of the American Indians* (London, 1775)

(Courtesy Huntington Library)

The Appalachian
Indian Frontier

THE EDMOND ATKIN

REPORT AND PLAN OF 1755

Edited with an Introduction by

Wilbur R. Jacobs

UNIVERSITY OF NEBRASKA PRESS · LINCOLN

First Bison Book printing September, 1967

Western
Americana

E
91
A87
1967

TO

MY MOTHER

AND

FATHER

*"It is proper, at all Times, to have a
watchful and attentive Eye upon Indian Affairs"*

James Glen, Governor of South Carolina, 1743-1756

Preface

The conquest of the colonial southwest was of momentous consequence in the history of this nation, for the rescue of vast areas of the hinterland helped in part to prepare the way for the independence of the British colonies. Yet to the Indian tribes along the southern frontier the westward advance of the Anglo-American population spelled disaster. If the French had been able to hold their interior forts, the downfall of the Indian would have been long delayed. In the 1750's, however, the French found themselves challenged all along the southern colonial frontier by an aggressive English trading advance. While the ensuing French and Indian War was a historical drama filled with tragic interest, it is also a period of no little obscurity on the western frontiers of the southern colonies.

Indian affairs were extremely important matters in colonial times; and large portions of provincial legislative journals and official communications are devoted to problems relating to the tribesmen. Yet close examination of the manuscripts and the printed sources concerning the southern frontier of the 1750's discloses much confusion and conflict in Indian diplomacy. Until the time of the outbreak of the French and Indian War, the control of Indian politics was in the hands of the various provincial governments—an unsatisfactory arrangement because of intercolonial rivalry in Indian affairs and in the fur trade.

Edmond Atkin, a member of the South Carolina Governor's Council and a merchant with long experience in the Indian trade, was aware of this situation. He had a scheme to place all Indian affairs under two imperial superintendents, one for the North and another for the South. Although this plan was not original with Atkin, his comprehensive report of 1755 and his plan were primarily responsible for his being elevated to the post of southern Indian superintendent in 1756. He faced the responsibilities of his new position with courage and determination and was loyal to his mother country, but died realizing that his work was not successful.

Atkin's writings, however, help to enlighten a whole period in American history that is in many respects unreclaimed. He tells the story of the "Vagabond Horse Pedlars" in their avid search for profits among the remoter tribes of the lower Mississippi Valley. Those hardy, rude men, traders and hunters, who ranged the southern wilderness beyond the frontiers of the colonies, formed a connecting link between civilization and barbarism. Atkin's descriptions of the Indian tribes, with their painted war sticks and fluttering trophies, throw light on a shadowy epoch that passed quickly from the American scene. His design for the superintendency system should be recognized as nothing less than a scheme to extend British imperial authority over an untamed wilderness in face of the rivalry of another major colonial power. Moreover, this plan for Indian management aids in explaining the evolution of an important imperial office in the history of colonial America. Both the historian and the ethnologist will find Atkin's writings useful in their researches.

As to acknowledgments, I owe a heavy debt of gratitude to my wife, whose help and criticisms have done much to bring about the completion of this work. To the late Professor Louis Knott Koontz of the University of California, Los Angeles, I am under obligation for the encouragement and advice that he generously extended to me at all times. My thanks are due to Miss Norma B. Cuthbert of the Division of Manuscripts in the Henry E. Huntington Library, whose wide knowledge of the Library's collections was put at my disposal. I am also grateful to the Huntington Library for permission to publish the Atkin manuscript. Mr. Ryde John of the Manuscript Room in the British Museum and Mr. Kenneth Timings of the Round Room in the Public Record Office courteously extended the facilities of their depositories to me while I was in London. The late Grace Gardner Griffin of the Division of Manuscripts in the Library of Congress and Mr. William Kaye Lamb, Dominion Archivist of the Public Archives of Canada, assisted me in the location of necessary documents. Mrs. Louise Jones DuBose, Director of the University of South Carolina Press, Mr. Charles E. Lee, Editor at the Press, Dr. J. H. Easterby, Director of the Historical Commission of South Carolina, and Dr. Robert L. Meriwether, Director of the South Caroliniana Library, gave counsel and assistance. Dr. John Richard Alden, Dr. Chapman J. Milling, and Dr. Charles W. Paape, scholars of southern colonial history, have kindly given me the benefit of their advice.

The library staffs on the various campuses of the University of California have fully cooperated in helping me secure essential materials. Dr. Donald C. Davidson, Mrs. Violet E. Shue, Mr. Hobart F. Berolzheimer, and Miss Debora King have given me all the assistance within their power.

Acknowledgments for financial assistance during the four-year period of preparation for this work are due primarily to the University of California Santa Barbara College Research Committee and also to Stanford University.

Material based upon the Introduction has appeared in the *Journal of Southern History*.

W. R. J.

*University of California
Santa Barbara College
June 9, 1953*

Contents

Illustrations

INTRODUCTION: EDMOND ATKIN

IMPERIAL INDIAN SUPERINTENDENT

The [southern] Natives are strong, lively, and well-shapen People, well humour'd, and generally kind to the English. They live a long and pleasant life, taking little care for the future. Their old Women plant their Mayz: And for the rest, the Rivers afford them good fish enough. And in the Woods, they have plenty of Provisions.[1]

The conflict which in America was called the French and Indian War, and in Europe the Seven Years' War, was the last of a series of four wars which culminated in the maritime and colonial preponderance of England over her European rivals. This imperial struggle made England the first of commercial powers and prepared for a vast colonial expansion that scattered British culture to every part of the globe. The Seven Years' War blighted France as a colonial power and almost crippled her commercial life. It gave England mastery of the seas and control over a huge wilderness of imperial dimensions in North America.

In 1748 the contestants, France and England, had terminated their third intercolonial war by the Treaty of Aix-la-Chapelle. This treaty proved to be only a truce, for after a few short years of troubled peace and diplomatic rivalry among the Indians, the French struck a new blow. In June, 1752, a swift force of Canadians and Indians swooped down upon the British trading outpost at Pickawillany on the Miami. The captive traders who were left alive were plundered to the skin, the village was destroyed, and Old Britain, the famous Miami chief, was boiled and eaten before the very eyes of his confederates.[2] Despite more than a century of Jesuit influence, the northern tribes had not entirely lost their taste for human flesh.[3] It appeared that peace must be won with the sword.

In the next year France asserted her claim to the hinterlands of the continent by moving troops to the sources of the Ohio to entrench herself at the gateway to the West. Recognizing this threat, Lieutenant Governor Robert Dinwiddie of Virginia, that staunch defender of the British royal prerogative, determined to force the French to a showdown, and in the fall of 1753 sent young George Washington on his historic journey to warn the French that

---

[1] "A New Map of Virginia, Maryland . . . and Carolina," John Thornton and Robert Morden (London, [1690?]) Public Record Office, Colonial Office (hereafter cited as P.R.O., C.O.), Map 1144. See descriptions of Indians on this map.

[2] Draper MSS, Wisconsin State Historical Society, Nos. 1 JJ 3-1 JJ 6, pp. 3-6; P.R.O., C.O., 5/1327.

[3] Cannibalism among the northern Indians was ceremonial rather than routine. Francis Parkman wrote that the Jesuits did their utmost to stamp it out. See his comments in *The Jesuits in North America in the Seventeenth Century* (Boston, 1893), pp. xxxix, xl, 248.

they were fortifying lands belonging to the English. Then followed the skirmish with Jumonville, and later the capitulation of Washington at Fort Necessity. The young commander began his humiliating retreat on the fourth of July, 1754, not realizing that he was to help make that date a great one for a newborn nation.[4]

One year later the British suffered a greater defeat. In the forest near the river Monongahela a powerful army under the dogged Major General Edward Braddock was fiercely attacked by a force of some six hundred Indians and two hundred and twenty Canadians and French soldiers, who left the British with a routed army, a dying general, and the rising leadership of George Washington.[5] After Braddock's demise there burst upon the frontier of 1755 a storm of blood and fire. Most of the Indians joined the victorious French, and not a British flag waved beyond the Appalachian mountains from Pennsylvania to the Carolinas.[6]

Confusion and maladministration in Indian affairs were partly responsible for the British predicament. It was fortunate indeed that Edward Braddock had appointed the able William Johnson as superintendent of Indian affairs for the North before the disaster on the Monongahela, for Johnson was able to prevent most of the Iroquois from later joining Montcalm.[7] While Johnson thus saved the northern colonies from what appeared to be a military calamity, danger of attack nevertheless still threatened from the South, where numerous warriors were considering the feasibility of combining forces with the enemy. A plan of management for Indian affairs might forestall the possible alienation of the Cherokee, the Chickasaw, the Creeks, and their allies.

Into this depressing scene strode Edmond Atkin, Charleston merchant of the Indian trade, whose career is a most interesting story of success and failure in provincial America. Chiefly as a result of his writings on Indian affairs, particularly his well-organized scheme of Indian management which he submitted to the Board of Trade in 1755, Atkin suddenly appeared as a leading colonial official, the newly appointed southern superintendent of the Indians. From the time of his appointment in 1756, however, until his death in 1761, Atkin's importance as an actor in the drama of Indian diplomacy in the French and Indian War steadily declined. Although he negotiated a

---

[4] Terms of the capitulation are found in Samuel Hazard (ed.), *Pennsylvania Archives* . . . (1st series), II (Philadelphia, 1853), 146-47.

[5] Winthrop Sargent (ed.), *The History of an Expedition against Fort Du Quesne in 1755* . . . (*Memoirs of the Historical Society of Pennsylvania*, Vol. V [Philadelphia, 1856]), p. 409.

[6] For a discussion concerning Indian affairs after Braddock's defeat, see Wilbur R. Jacobs, *Diplomacy and Indian Gifts, Anglo-French Rivalry along the Ohio and Northwest Frontiers, 1748-1763* (Stanford, Calif., 1950), pp. 145 ff.

[7] Johnson's efforts at this time were devoted to keeping the majority of the Iroquois neutral. See James Sullivan *et al.* (eds.), *The Papers of Sir William Johnson* (New York, 1921——) (hereafter cited as *Johnson Papers*), III, 269-75.

number of successful treaties with the southern tribes and was instrumental in bringing warriors to aid Washington in 1757 and General John Forbes in 1758, Atkin's work was soon forgotten by his countrymen. Recently his career has been examined by such scholars as John Carl Parish, and, later, John Richard Alden and Douglas Freeman; but Atkin is usually regarded as a failure.[8]

Much of the condemnation stems from the criticisms which were hurled at Atkin by his contemporaries. With Scotch frugality, Governor Dinwiddie of Virginia complained about Atkin's "monstrous Acco't of Expenses" and charged that the superintendent was "very slow in all his Affairs." The Indian trader James Adair had no kind words for Atkin, declaring that the superintendent trifled away his time and showed little or no knowledge of Indian politics. Even George Washington's patience was exhausted because of Atkin's constant delays in providing supplies for Indian "fighting men." [9]

The superintendent was not unaware of the biting criticisms made by his fellow-provincials. With much good reason he shifted blame for his early inactivity to the shoulders of the Earl of Loudoun, who seemed to be too preoccupied with his business as commander-in-chief of British forces to bother with Atkin's work or financial problems. In a sense, the superintendent's want of success mirrored the shortcomings of his superior, the Earl of Loudoun, of whom Benjamin Franklin wrote in his *Autobiography*, ". . . he is like St. George on the signs, *always on horseback, and never rides on.*" Although Atkin did little in haste, and his actions were usually characterized by measured deliberation, he was further handicapped by lack of financial support from the mother country. In a letter to William Pitt in 1760 Atkin bitterly charged that he had courageously carried on his duties for four years without a "Shilling of the King's Money." Meantime, he said, his enemies had "hatcheted" his reputation worse than his head had been scarified by an Indian warrior.[10]

Atkin also had certain failings in personality. In his jealous attempts to extend his authority over all persons who had any contact with the southern Indians and their allies, he was lacking in tact and discretion and quarreled with William Johnson's deputies and the colonial governors. In his dealings with the tribesmen, he made the error of being pompous and overbearing.

---

[8] John Carl Parish, *The Persistence of the Westward Movement and Other Essays,* ed. Louis Knott Koontz (Berkeley, Calif., 1943), pp. 147-60; John Richard Alden, *John Stuart and the Southern Colonial Frontier* . . . (Ann Arbor, Mich., 1944), pp. 68-70, 134-35; Douglas Southall Freeman, *George Washington, A Biography,* II (New York, 1948), 247 ff.

[9] John C. Fitzpatrick (ed.), *The Writings of George Washington from the Original Manuscript Sources, 1745-1799* (Washington, D. C., 1931-1944) (hereafter cited as *Writings of Washington*), I, 36, 39.

[10] Edmond Atkin to William Pitt, March 27, 1760, P.R.O., C.O., 5/64.

His lack of diplomatic finesse caused the Indians on occasion to doubt his statements. When he told the Choctaw that "When my King has a mind to Attack the French, he will send his Great Ships & Warriors . . ." the Indians burst into laughter and replied, "We wish we could hear & see that." [11] In another instance, according to James Adair, a warrior named Tobacco Eater, in a violent eruption of anger during a conference, almost severed the superintendent's scalp from his head.[12] Indeed, Atkin's faults were not concealed from the Indians or from his fellow-provincials.

Yet his slow, meticulous labors in organizing his department of Indian affairs constitute a significant chapter in early frontier history, and his plan for Indian management, the first comprehensive one submitted to the Board of Trade, was an outstanding achievement. It is obvious from Atkin's writings that he had much firsthand knowledge concerning Indian affairs. His report and plan of 1755 were based upon some twenty years of experience as a merchant and as a member of the Council in dealing with Indians and Indian traders. These points, rather than his failures, should be emphasized.

Edmond Atkin was born in England in 1707, but, as he once mentioned in an Indian conference, he had lived in South Carolina ever since his boyhood.[13] During the 1730's with one John Atkin, probably his brother, he established a trading concern in Charleston.[14] This venture was so successful that by the year 1738 Edmond had achieved enough recognition to be honored with a seat on the South Carolina Governor's Council.[15]

Atkin once declared that while acting as one of "the Great King George's Counsellors" for eighteen years he had become acquainted with many of the

---

[11] See Atkin's conferences with the Choctaw in October, 1759, in P.R.O., C.O., 5/64.

[12] Samuel Cole Williams (ed.), *Adair's History of the American Indians* (Johnson City, Tenn., 1930), p. 270. Adair speaks of Atkin's "pride, obstinacy, and unskilfulness."

[13] For Atkin's birth, see Alden, *John Stuart*, p. 68. The citation given is W. U. Upham and H. Tapley-Soper (eds.), *The Registers of Baptisms, Marriages, & Burials of the City of Exeter* (Exeter, England, 1910-1933), II, 45. Atkin's will mentions a brother and five sisters living near Exeter. It is probable that the John Atkin who shared a business and certain land holdings was also a brother. The will is found in Charleston County, South Carolina, Record of Wills, Vol. 9 (1760-1767), pp. 199-200. For the Indian conference mentioned above, see E. B. O'Callaghan *et al.* (eds.), *Documents Relative to the Colonial History of the State of New York* . . . (Albany, 1853-1887) (hereafter cited as *New York Colonial Documents*), VII, 211.

[14] Records of the business activities of John and Edmond Atkin are found in J. H. Easterby (ed.), *The Colonial Records of South Carolina: The Journal of the Commons House of Assembly* (Columbia, S.C., 1951——) (hereafter cited as *S.C. Assembly Journals*), September 12, 1739—March 26, 1741, pp. 112, 228. See also "Council Journals" (MSS, Historical Commission of South Carolina), Vol. IX (1742-1743), p. 44; Pre-Revolutionary Land Plat Folders (MSS, Historical Commission of South Carolina); Verner W. Crane, *The Southern Frontier, 1670-1732* (Durham, N.C., 1928), p. 121.

[15] Huntington Library Collection of Loudoun Papers, No. 578, p. 1 (p. 3, below). This is the manuscript which contains the report and plan for Indian control of 1755. (All Loudoun papers are hereafter cited as LO.)

"head men" of the southern Indian nations.[16] When the warrior delegations came to Charleston to confer with the governor and his Council, Atkin, according to his writings, took a deep interest in the affairs of native diplomacy. He learned all that was possible about Indians, their problems, the abuses of the fur trade, and the rivalry between the French and the English for the affection of the tribesmen.

Atkin's record in the South Carolina Council also shows him to be a vigorous defender of royal interests. He lamented the loss of opportunities to establish "the British interest to the Banks of the Mississippi River, & the Bay of Mexico." He was an alert observer of what he thought were encroachments on the part of the French, and he hoped to weaken Britain's enemy by interfering with her trade in the "Sugar Islands." Furthermore, the future superintendent was outspoken in his protests against measures like "the Emission of Paper Currency" which were "highly displeasing to our Mother Country." Atkin's interests as councilor were also directed toward military defense, regulation of the Indian trade, tax measures, and encouraging "poor Protestants to become Settlers" in South Carolina.[17] In March, 1743, he was nominated by the Upper House for the position of Public Treasurer of the Colony, but declined the honor because it would have necessitated his resignation from the Council and "private affairs also might in a short time require his presence in England. . . ."[18]

From the evidence in the Council Journals and the Upper House Journals one suspects that Atkin considered himself more of an Englishman than a provincial.[19] It is not surprising that councilor Atkin frequently found himself in disagreement with the Lower House. On one occasion "warm words" passed between Atkin and one Andrew Rutledge, a member of the Assembly. Atkin vehemently protested that he was charged "with Words never spoken." This affair, which occurred in March, 1740, caused an extraordinary uproar. The Upper House would not meet with the Lower House until "Satisfaction" had been given to the disgruntled councilor. At length, following a report of an Assembly committee, appointed to reply to the Council on the

---

[16] *New York Colonial Documents,* VII, 211.

[17] *S. C. Assembly Journals, 1739-1741,* pp. 40, 56, 220, 264, 439 ff.; "Council Journals," Vol. VII (1737-1741), pp. 353-55, 360; Anne King Gregorie (ed.), *Records of the Court of the Chancery of South Carolina, 1671-1799* (Washington, D. C., 1950), pp. 390 ff.

[18] "Council Journals," Vol. IX (1742-1743), pp. 56-57.

[19] Atkin's vigorous opposition to the Assembly's bills which he thought were contrary to the Crown's interest is clearly brought out in the Council Journals of the 1740's. See, for example, "Council Journals," Vol. VII (1737-1741), pp. 353 ff. (Although the "Council Journals" and "Upper House Journals" are often entered in the same manuscript volumes, the volumes are labeled "Council Journals" and are thus cited here.)

dispute, Rutledge made a suitable apology which undoubtedly helped to soothe the future superintendent's ruffled feelings.[20]

This dispute illustrates the high esteem that Atkin had for his position as "Counsellor." He had scant regard for "Recommendations from popular Assemblies . . . *in exclusion* of the Council, tho supported by the Governor." Rather, Atkin declared, "His Majesty's Council in our several Colonies, being appointed by himself, sworn to do their Duty, & removable at Pleasure, are undoubtedly the *natural Guardians* there of his Prerogative, Rights, & Interest; and the surest Channel of true Information to the Crown or Ministry." [21]

An analysis of Atkin's writings further indicates that he was very dissatisfied with the manner in which South Carolina conducted its governmental affairs, particularly its Indian affairs. He doubtless felt it necessary that the British home government should have more "true information" concerning the conditions in the southern colonies. From his writings, one cannot escape the opinion that Atkin had a strong sense of duty and was firm in his convictions; and it is apparent that his discontent was strong enough to cause him to go to England where he might have the opportunity to present his views directly to the Board of Trade. He had been planning a voyage for some seven years because of "private affairs," however, and probably wished to visit relatives in Exeter. In 1750 he terminated his business connections and in October sailed for England, where he remained for six years.[22]

When he left the colonies, Atkin did not give up his seat in the Governor's Council. This peculiar situation caused the Board of Trade in 1754 to inquire if Atkin ever intended to return to South Carolina and resume his work. In the future superintendent's eyes there had been a number of "Dishonours to Government" in South Carolina, and he wrote that under these circumstances resignation would be "a kind of Desertion of my Post & Duty." He added that he was recuperating from illness and meantime was occupied in "Public Service" in England, probably referring to his principal writings upon Indian affairs, which appear to have been composed in London between 1750 and 1755.[23]

---

[20] *S.C. Assembly Journals, 1739-1741,* pp. 263-66. Rutledge's statement was not deemed a "Satisfaction," however. No further mention of the dispute is found in the Assembly Journals.

[21] Edmond Atkin, "Historical Account of the Revolt of the Chactaw Indians . . .," London, January 20, 1753, Lansdowne MSS (British Museum, London), 809, p. 32. (This document is hereafter cited as Atkin, "The Choctaw Revolt.")

[22] *Ibid.,* p. 23.

[23] It is possible that Atkin did some work on his writings while he was in South Carolina. The Choctaw revolt essay was finished on January 20, 1753, and the report and plan of 1755 was submitted on May 30, 1755. For the above quotes, see Edmond Atkin to John Pownall, June 8, 1754, P.R.O., C.O., 5/34; Atkin, "The Choctaw Revolt," p. 32.

While regaining his health in England, Atkin used his knowledge of
Indian politics to author two documents of substantial magnitude. The first
paper was a thirty-thousand-word history of the bloody Choctaw revolt of
1746, and the second was his report and scheme for imperial Indian control
of 1755. The memoir on the Choctaw revolt tells the story of the mass of
intrigue surrounding the activities of Red Shoes, a Choctaw war chief who
led a large faction of his people into alliance with the British because of
French shortcomings in the fur and skin trade. A storm of native politics
followed the diplomatic revolution of Red Shoes, with the result that the
French governor of Louisiana, Pierre de Rigaud, Marquis de Vaudreuil,[24]
demanded no less than the head of Red Shoes as a propitiation from the
Choctaw. Further complications came with the assassination of Red Shoes,
brought about by the French governor; and a general civil war broke out
among the unfortunate Choctaw, ending in the eventual defeat of the English
faction.

Atkin's essay gives a detailed account of how the Choctaw revolt was ex-
ploited by three South Carolinians: James Adair, fur trader and author of a
history of the Indians;[25] Charles McNaire, "a Stranger lately come to
Carolina . . . having met with Misfortune at Sea [but] . . . willing
to try his Luck on Shore . . ." in the Indian trade;[26] and James Glen,
governor of South Carolina.[27] All three receive a sound tongue-lashing for
promoting the civil war and then leaving their Indian allies with nothing to
fight with, except glass beads to be used as bullets! This memoir concerning
the Choctaw is further distinguished as containing clear reference to what
historians have suspected, that some of the French forts received supplies and
Indian goods from British traders.

Although the essay upon the Choctaw revolt is a formidable document,
packed with information relating to the fur and skin commerce, Edmond
Atkin's long report to the Board of Trade outlining his plan for the superintendencies is, of the two, the superior work. The latter document is out-

---

[24] Vaudreuil was governor of Louisiana from 1743 to 1753. For a complete sketch,
see Theodore Calvin Pease et al. (eds.), *Illinois on the Eve of the Seven Years' War,
1747-1755* (*Collections* of the Illinois State Historical Library, Vol. XXIX [Springfield,
1940]), pp. xix-xx.

[25] *Supra*, note 12. Indian Commissioner Major William Pinckney characterized Adair
as "a great Villain" in connection with the Choctaw revolt. See "Journals of the Commons House of Assembly" (MSS, South Carolina Historical Commission), Vol. XXV
1749-1750), pp. 683 ff.

[26] For criticisms of McNaire's conduct, see *ibid.*; Atkin, "The Choctaw Revolt,"
pp. 24 ff.

[27] Despite Atkin's criticisms, Glen is generally regarded as one of the outstanding
governors of the colonial period. He was a vigorous expansionist, and his interests
conflicted with those of Robert Dinwiddie, governor of Virginia. See Mary F. Carter,
"James Glen, Governor of South Carolina . . ." (Doctoral dissertation, University
of California, Los Angeles, 1951).

standing in terms of clarity of thought and general information regarding the status of the entire colonial Indian frontier, and no doubt the magnitude of Atkin's knowledge of Indian affairs sufficiently impressed the Board of Trade. After some gentle prodding of the Board on the part of the South Carolinian and, probably, the exercise of influence by his friends, he received his appointment in the spring of 1756 as "Agent for and Superintendent of" the Indian tribes bordering the southern colonies. This appointment was made with some misgivings, however, and the word "sole" which had appeared with "Superintendent" in William Johnson's commission was absent in Atkin's.[28] The Earl of Loudoun was even given final authority to approve Atkin's appointment. For instructions and money the Board of Trade referred the South Carolinian to the commander-in-chief who ". . . would doubtless upon application furnish him with whatever might be necessary. . . ."[29]

Atkin followed close upon the trail of Loudoun from England to New York, arriving on October 6, 1756. In dogged pursuit of the General, his travels took him to Albany, back to New York, then on to Boston, back to New York, and finally to Philadelphia before a satisfactory contact was made. The superintendent had been delayed in the North some five months because he had no "Dispatches with Instructions" from the General. In a letter from New York, and finally to Philadelphia before a satisfactory contact was made. grumbled:

> Methinks I see your Surprize at the place & Date of this Letter. You'll be more surprized when I tell you, that I returned last Thursday Morning from *Boston*. . . .
>
> As his Lordship set out for Boston on ye 10th of January, without giving them [instructions] to me, So considering the Time that must necessarily be lost till his Return, I came to a Resolution at once to follow him, in hopes that he might find that leisure there for the purpose which he did not here. . . . When I got to Boston, I found Lord Loudoun had not Some Necessary Papers with him. So after travelling since my first arrival here, by Land & Water above 900 Miles, through severest Frosts & Snow, & the worst Roads, behold here I am again just where I was on ye 6th of October; and will expect not to

---

[28] Johnson received his commission from Braddock on April 15, 1755, *Johnson Papers*, I, 465-66. Atkin's is dated May 13, 1756, P.R.O., C.O., 324/51, p. 87. Also see LO 1212; LO 559; LO 561. Braddock was also authorized to appoint a southern superintendent, but he did not exercise this power. See John Richard Alden, "The Albany Congress and the Creation of the Indian Superintendencies," *Mississippi Valley Historical Review*, Vol. XXVII, No. 2 (September, 1940), p. 208.

[29] *Journal of the Commissioners for Trade and Plantations from April 1704 to May 1782* (London, 1920-1938), X, 242-43. Also see Atkin's letter to Loudoun on May 14, 1756, concerning his salary, LO 1148.

JAMES GLEN, GOVERNOR OF SOUTH CAROLINA, 1743-1756

A Copy of an Eighteenth-Century Miniature

(Courtesy Mr. Glen Drayton Grimke, Charleston, S. C.)

receive my Dispatches till I reach Philadelphia, for which place his Lordship will set out I suppose in 3 or 4 days.[30]

In his interview with Loudoun at Philadelphia Atkin was undoubtedly disappointed that the General declined to give him the needed funds for Indian presents and the army of interpreters, gunsmiths, rangers, surgeons, clerks, and other assistants which he thought necessary for the operation of the southern department of Indian affairs. Finding himself dependent upon the southern colonies for financial support, the disappointed superintendent made a belated arrival in Williamsburg, Virginia, in the spring of 1757.[31] After considerable solicitation from the dynamic governor, Robert Dinwiddie, Atkin repaired to the Virginia frontier and established his headquarters at Fort Loudoun at Winchester, where he planned to confer with Indian warriors and to give them presents.[32]

During the spring of 1757, young Colonel George Washington, commanding the forces defending the wide Virginia frontier, had been having manifold difficulties in managing his Indian allies. The Cherokee, he indignantly declared, were "the most insolent, most avaricious, and most dissatisfied wretches I have ever had to deal with." [33] No one realized more fully than the youthful commander that gifts of wampum, spirits, strouds (a cheap woolen cloth made of rags used for clothing and blankets), hardware, and ornaments were a necessity in dealing with Indians. Without these presents, the warriors would become surly and desert their allies.

Responsibility for the capricious, churlish Indians now devolved upon Atkin. After his delayed arrival at Winchester on June 3, 1757, the superintendent began a long series of intricate negotiations with the Cherokee, the Catawba, and other tribesmen, placating them with suitable gifts.[34] During the summer of this year he was fortunate to secure the assistance of several subordinates, including the experienced Maryland frontiersman and surveyor, Christopher Gist,[35] who acted as his deputy. However, the superintendent

---

[30] P.R.O., C.O., 323/13. In addition see Atkin's long memorandums to Loudoun during October and November of 1756, LO 1979, LO 2045, and LO 2282. Loudoun's "Memorandum Books," in almost indecipherable handwriting, preserved in the Huntington Library, have references to Atkin.

[31] R[obert] A. Brock (ed.), *The Official Records of Robert Dinwiddie* . . . (Virginia Historical Society *Collections*, n. s., Vols. III and IV [Richmond, 1883-1884]) (hereafter cited as Brock, *Dinwiddie Papers*), II, 616-17. Also see Louis Knott Koontz (ed.), *Robert Dinwiddie Correspondence* . . . (Berkeley, Calif., 1951), pp. 1015-16, 1232.

[32] For the location of the fort, see Louis Knott Koontz, *The Virginia Frontier, 1754-1763* (Baltimore, 1925), pp. 129-30; Freeman, *George Washington*, II, 229.

[33] *Writings of Washington*, II, 36-37.

[34] Atkin arrived in Winchester late on June 2 or on June 3, 1757. See *ibid.*, p. 44; Koontz, *Dinwiddie Correspondence*, p. 1242.

[35] For Gist's instructions see LO 3990; P.R.O., War Office, 34/47. Atkin had several other assistants who acted as interpreters and "conductors" for the Indians. See LO 3589.

managed to quarrel with Johnson's chief assistant, George Croghan,[36] and to send bristling epistles to several of the colonial governors.

To Atkin's credit, he strongly condemned the practice of paying bounties to the Indians for scalps. On June 30, 1757, he wrote to Governor Horatio Sharpe of Maryland:

> It remains only for me to say something concerning Scalps. I find several of our Colonies are become fond of giving large Rewards for them. If these Rewards were confined to their own people, it would be a very laudable thing, inasmuch as it would be the means of animating many poor white Men, who have been used to the Woods, to go in Quest of Enemy Indians, and it would afford that support to some of them in particular, who have been driven from their own Habitations in the back settlements, by the War, which they are certainly the best entitled to. But as those Rewards are intended & offered chiefly to Indians, the Case is very different. For besides that this is truly & literally interfering (which I have Reason to believe the several Governors have been cautioned not to do) with the Management of the King's two Superintendents, through whose hands all Presents & Rewards whatever to the Indians in his Alliance ought to pass, it is encouraging to the utmost *private Scalping*, whereby the most innocent & helpless Persons, even Women & Children, are properly murdered, without the least Benefit accruing by it; Actions only becoming the greatest Savages, & unworthy of any Christian People to reward. I am well assured Lord Loudoun detests that practice, and that the French General Mon[t]calm in Canada does the same. Sir Wm. Johnson gives no Reward at all in particular for Scalps by name. The Warriours fitted out by him to War, deliver to him at their Return all that they bring back; and he afterwards presents them to the Relations of such as lose their Lives in Battle. I should be ashamed not to follow such good Examples. But to speak upon this Subject on the footing of Interest, large publick Rewards for Scalps given by Provincial Laws to Indians, are attended with very pernicious Consequences to his Majesty's Service; for they are so many Temptations to some Indians to kill others that are our Friends; that is when they think they have a good Opportunity to kill such single Indians that are found alone.[37]

The conventional method of rewarding Indian auxiliaries for successful attacks on the enemy was to allot presents according to the number of scalps and prisoners obtained by the triumphant warriors. Washington was aided

---

[36] Albert T. Volwiler, *George Croghan and the Westward Movement, 1741-1782* (Cleveland, 1926), pp. 129-30; *Minutes of the Provincial Council of Pennsylvania . . .* (Philadelphia, 1851-1858), VII, 598.

[37] *Pennsylvania Archives* (1st series), III, 199.

by Indian "fighting men" like Warhatchie, chief of all the southern Cherokee towns, and the Swallow, a belligerent war chief. These Indians were fierce warriors, fighting primarily for gifts of blankets and hardware. Warhatchie, called by Atkin "the greatest rogue" among the Cherokee because of his mercenary interest in presents, allowed his men to act like "Free Booters in an Enemy Country." [38] The violence and plundering of such truculent, belli-cose Indians was not always directed toward the enemy. Indeed, the super-intendent's stalwart efforts to call a halt to the buying of scalps deserve much commendation.

Surrounded by warlike savages, Atkin found it difficult to distinguish be-tween friends and enemies. To rectify the situation he established a system of "passports" for friendly Indians.[39] His stern manner in time helped to bring a semblance of order out of the confusion; but once he went too far. In July, 1757, he imprisoned ten warriors whose insolent air gave him the impression they were French spies. This incident almost caused a rupture with the Cherokee, much to the consternation of Washington, who sent a messenger to the Cherokee towns indicating that the whole affair was a mistake. Although the superintendent heaped presents upon the prisoners and assured them that no "hurt was intended," his untimely action enraged the warriors at Winchester and complicated Washington's military problems.[40]

Conditions relating to Indian affairs gradually improved, nevertheless, and by August, 1757, Dinwiddie concluded that the Indians were behaving "pretty well"—an indication that Atkin's negotiations on the Virginia frontier were not entirely unsatisfactory to the governor.[41]

One reason why Atkin was able to placate Washington's Indian allies was that the Virginia government gave the superintendent excellent financial support. Though a portion of the money in Governor Dinwiddie's hands was an allotment from the Crown, large outlays by the House of Burgesses punc-tuate the correspondence of the governor during this period. Pennsylvania and Maryland failed, for the most part, in responding to Atkin's call for funds, with the result that Virginia had to bear most of the financial burden for Indian presents. Even though relations with the Indians had improved, the matter of the superintendent's "monstrous Acco't of Expenses" in Virginia

---

[38] Edmond Atkin to George Croghan, June 8, 1757, *ibid.*, pp 175-81.

[39] Atkin had made previous arrangements with the Iroquois and Sir William Johnson concerning his "passports." See *New York Colonial Documents,* VII, 211-15. A repro-duction of Atkin's seal which appeared upon the passports is found in the *South-Carolina Gazette,* March 29 to April 7, 1760.

[40] For accounts of this incident, see *Writings of Washington,* II, 97, 115; Edmond Atkin to the Commander of Fort Prince George, July 22, 1757, "Indian Books of South Carolina" (MSS, Historical Commission of South Carolina), Vol. VI, pp. 81-83.

[41] Brock, *Dinwiddie Papers,* II, 689. For Atkin's expense accounts in Virginia, see Jacobs, *Diplomacy and Indian Gifts,* pp. 64-65, 164-65; Stanley M. Pargellis, *Lord Loudoun in North America* (New Haven, Conn., 1933), pp. 258-59.

caused raised eyebrows on the part of Dinwiddie and the council in October, 1757. Relations between the old Scot and Atkin were further strained when the superintendent quarreled with Dinwiddie about regulations concerning Indian commerce.[42]

Although Atkin planned to journey southward to make treaties with the tribesmen on the South Carolina frontier, his departure was probably hastened by the hostility that developed with Dinwiddie. Before leaving Winchester in the fall of 1757, Atkin made arrangements for Christopher Gist to act as his deputy in Virginia. In March, 1758, delayed because of illness in New Bern, North Carolina, and also by habitual reluctance for hasty action, he finally arrived in Charleston to begin a series of treaties with the southern Indians.[43] Despite the fact that the serious state of Cherokee affairs appears to have merited the personal attention of Atkin, he allowed William Byrd of the Virginia council, his newly appointed assistant, to negotiate with these tribesmen. The superintendent then contented himself with "applications" to the Cherokee and recommendations to Byrd. These measures were some help in raising a force of warriors to aid General John Forbes in the campaign of 1758.[44] Atkin defended his inactivity in a letter to the Board of Trade by pointing out that his horses had been "reduced extremely low in condition." Moreover, both William Byrd and Governor William Henry Lyttelton, who had succeeded James Glen as governor of South Carolina, agreed, according to Atkin, that the journey to the Cherokee town of Keowee by the superintendent was unnecessary at this time.[45]

During the early summer of 1758 no less than six hundred friendly Cherokee, lured northward by William Byrd's watered rum and presents, came to the aid of the Forbes army. The march of the army toward Fort Duquesne, however, was delayed in part by Loudoun's shifting of regiments, and the disappointed warriors accused the British of being "Trifflers" and went home.[46] Atkin's collaboration with Byrd had been successful; but the complicated British troop maneuvers temporarily stalled the Forbes offensive in the middle colonies.

[42] Edmond Atkin to Nathaniel Walthoe, January 26, 175[8], P.R.O., War Office, 34/47. See Brock, *Dinwiddie Papers*, II, 707, for the quotation on Atkin's expenses in Virginia.

[43] Atkin wrote to Loudoun on March 25, 1758, stating that he had been delayed in New Bern, North Carolina, because of illness. See Abercromby Papers, Huntington Library (hereafter cited as AB), No. 73.

[44] Loudoun appointed Byrd to assist Atkin. See Pargellis, *Lord Loudoun in North America*, pp. 258-59.

[45] AB 73. For Byrd's work with the Cherokee, see AB 70; LO 5776; Stanley M. Pargellis (ed.), *Military Affairs in North America, 1748-1765* . . . (New York, 1936), p. 431. Also see Alfred Proctor James (ed. and comp.), *Writings of General John Forbes* . . . (Menasha, Wis., 1938), pp. 41 ff.

[46] Pargellis, *Military Affairs in North America*, p. 431.

Meanwhile, Atkin concerned himself with South Carolina affairs in Charleston. He desired to be on hand when the Assembly met in April, 1758, and during the spring and summer of this year he served as President of the South Carolina Council. These activities prevented him from giving his undivided attention to Indian affairs, and it was not until July of 1759 that he rode into the Creek towns, escorted by rangers from the colony of Georgia.[47] From July to November, 1759, he labored in the Upper Creek country, cementing alliances and trading agreements with the Creeks, the Choctaw, and the "Albahma Indians commonly called the Stinking Lingua Indians." [48] He obtained the promise of the tribesmen that they would not molest British traders or "Carry or send the French Talks." Atkin also announced that he did not approve of buying scalps, "having any hand in Blood," indicating that he was still trying to put a stop to this barbarous practice which persisted in the British colonies. Although the superintendent, according to the Creeks, had "nothing but good talks" with them, he was not, however, able to win the allegiance of two key war chiefs, Gun Merchant and The Mortar. These belligerent war leaders, were to be a problem for British Indian diplomats for some time.

Atkin later maintained that his conferences, messages, and "talks" prevented the Creeks and other southern tribesmen from joining the Cherokee in their bloody war against the British in 1760-1761; but his curious neglect of Cherokee affairs opens much room for criticism in connection with the origin of the conflict. Atkin was not idle after his return to Charleston on March 24, 1760, however. He aided the Governor's Council in its preparations for a military campaign against the Indians, and then joined the army of Lieutenant Colonel Archibald Montgomery as it slowly moved toward the lower Cherokee towns in June.

It is known that Atkin went into the Cherokee country as far as Fort Prince George in July, 1760. The *South-Carolina Gazette* reported that he was with wounded soldiers at that fort on July 5; but this excursion appears to be his main action in connection with the Cherokee War.[49] Later in July he negotiated a treaty with the Catawba Indians; and this was probably his final official act as superintendent.

During the late summer news arrived in Charleston of the Cherokee butchery of Fort Loudoun's soldiers, which followed the capitulation and

---

[47] For Atkin's journey to Savannah, his conference with the Georgia council and Governor Henry Ellis, and his later trip to Fort Moore, escorted by twelve rangers, see Allen D. Candler (ed.), *Colonial Records of the State of Georgia* (Atlanta, 1904-1916), VII, 826-27.

[48] P.R.O., C.O., 5/34. The "Stinkard" language differed from the Muskogee.

[49] Alden, *John Stuart*, p. 133. Also see. B. R. Carroll (ed. and comp.), *Historical Collections of South Carolina* (New York, 1836), I, 456.

abandonment of this fort in the heart of the Overhill country.[50] It was a great victory for the Indians but a savage one, as the barbarous deaths that met unfortunate Captain Paul Demeré and his men indicate.[51] Fortunately, the capable John Stuart,[52] later Atkin's successor as superintendent, was ransomed from his captors by Attakullakulla, long-time friend of the English and famous chief of the Cherokee.[53]

Atkin's last year of correspondence is filled with discontent and disillusionment. In defense of his failures he wrote that the governors, seeking to enhance their reputations as managers of Indian affairs, all but ignored him; the traders undermined him with acrimonious lies; the provincial assemblies were jealous of his powers; and Governor Henry Ellis of Georgia accorded him "cruel Treatment." Atkin, in truth, had little cause or desire to continue in "this invidious Office." [54] Added misfortunes were that he had expended personal funds without compensation and that his health was poor.[55]

Though near the end of his years, Atkin had briefly turned his attention away from Indian affairs to marry the daughter of a Scotch nobleman early in

---

[50] For a full account of the fall of Fort Loudoun, see Alden, *John Stuart*, pp. 114-18. Fort Loudoun, on the southern bank of the Little Tennessee, is not to be confused with the fort at Winchester or the fort build by Major Andrew Lewis' Virginians. Volume V of the "Indian Books of South Carolina" includes letters from Captain Raymond Demeré relating to the construction of the South Carolina fort in 1756. The Lewis fort was built near the Cherokee town of "Chotte." See *ibid.*, pp. 152-53, 157. For reference to the exact location of the South Carolina fort, see *ibid.*, p. 270.

[51] Captain Paul Demeré, who met his death while commanding Fort Loudoun, is not to be confused with his older brother, Raymond, who commanded troops which built the fort. See, Alden, *John Stuart*, pp. 57-60, 118; Robert L. Meriwether, *The Expansion of South Carolina, 1729-1765* (Kingsport, Tenn., 1940), pp. 213-14, 217.

[52] John Stuart was southern superintendent from 1763 to 1779. Robert Rogers, famous frontiersman and ranger leader, applied for the position after Atkin's death. See "Memorial of Robert Rogers," October 24, 1761, P.R.O., War Office, 34/47.

[53] Attakullakulla, or Little Carpenter, noted Cherokee chief, was probably the Indian youth in the Cherokee embassy which visited London in 1730. See Crane, *Southern Frontier*, p. 279. A sketch appears in Frederick Webb Hodge (ed.), *Handbook of the American Indians North of Mexico* (Washington, D. C., 1907), I, 115.

[54] Edmond Atkin to Jeffrey Amherst, November 20, 1760, P.R.O., War Office, 34/47. See also Helen Louise Shaw, *British Administration of the Southern Indians, 1756-1783* (Lancaster, Pa., 1931), pp. 9-15 ff.

[55] In almost all his correspondence Atkin makes reference to illness. Undoubtedly the rigors of the superintendency had much to do with his death at fifty-four. However, Professor John R. Alden in his *John Stuart*, p. 135 n., writes: "Dr. Alexander Garden, a Charleston physician personally acquainted with Atkin, wrote in 1758: '. . . how far the design and import of that appointment [of Atkin] will be answered by a man whose sole business is to cook good dinners for himself in Charlestown, time, and probably the defection of some one or other of these [Indian] nations, will shew.'" The citation given is: Garden to John Ellis, August 11, 1758, Sir James Edward Smith (ed.), *A Selection of the Correspondence of Linnaeus, and Other Naturalists . . .* (London, 1821), I, 427.

The total amount claimed by Atkin was £954 18s. 4½d. See Lady Anne Atkin to the "Lords Commissioners of his Majesty's Treasury," British Museum, Additional Manuscript, 38334, pp. 133-36. The manuscript is torn and difficult to read. Also see LO 6350.

May of 1760.[56] His marital bliss was short lived, however. On May 22, 1760, he signed his will, and, after a lingering illness following a visit to the frontier during the Cherokee War, died on October 8, 1761, at his plantation on the Pee Dee River.[57]

Although his arrogance and obvious ineptitude unfitted him for the post of Indian superintendent, much blame for Atkin's limited success can be traced to the British home government. Even a talented Indian diplomat like Sir William Johnson needed financial backing and strong governmental support to carry on his work as superintendent. It was an error to appoint Atkin in the first place; but it was a grievous mistake to leave him to his own devices once he had assumed the office. The result was that Indian affairs, for the most part, remained in the hands of southern governors during Atkin's superintendency.

Despite the fact that evidence is fragmentary, several additional conclusions can be made. It is reasonable to deduce that Atkin made a serious attempt to organize a far-flung Indian department that included a scattered native population spread out along the frontier from Maryland to Georgia. There was no confederacy of Indian "nations" like the Iroquois to serve as a focal point of administration for the southern department. Moreover, Atkin molded his foundation for the southern superintendency despite great provincial opposition. A pioneer in the vexing problems of his office, he represented imperial authority in relations with the southern governors, the assemblies, and vested interests engaged in Indian commerce.[58] True, Atkin's foundation was weak, but his work undoubtedly established precedents which aided John Stuart when the latter assumed office in 1763.[59] Atkin's attempt to extend the authority of his office over the southern fur trading interests is in part a prelude to later developments in imperial regulation.

The extreme reluctance of the Earl of Loudoun to provide financial assistance for the southern Indian department undermined any real hope for Atkin's

---

[56] D. E. Huger Smith and Alexander S. Salley, Jr. (eds.), *Register of St. Philip's Parish, Charles Town or Charleston, S. C., 1754-1810* (Charleston, 1927), p. 158. Lady Atkin was the daughter of the Earl of Cromartie. She later married Dr. John Murray on February 18, 1764, A. S. Salley, Jr. (ed. and comp.), *Marriage Notices in the South-Carolina Gazette and Its Successors (1732-1801)* (Albany, N. Y., 1902), p. 26. For the story of the Cromartie family, see Lord Dover (ed.), *Letters of Horace Walpole . . .* (London, 1834), II, 149, 153, 158.

[57] A. S. Salley, Jr. (ed. and comp.), *Death Notices in the South Carolina Gazette, 1732-1775* (Columbia, S. C., 1917), p. 29.

[58] He was especially handicapped because the office of the superintendency had no special rank in the hierarchy of the imperial colonial system. Atkin, however, was shrewd enough to keep his position on the Council of South Carolina, preside during his term of presidency, and remain a member of the "Court of Chancery." See "Council Journals," Vol. XXVI (1757-1758), p. 143.

[59] Stuart's problems in dealing with the traders were quite similar to those of Atkin. See, for example, John Stuart to John Pownall, August 24, 1765, Shelburne Papers, W. L. Clements Library, Vol. 60, pp. 39-67.

success. Loudoun was apparently convinced, and with good reason, that the vital theater of war was in the North; therefore, the General had little regard for the military importance of the major Indian tribes of the South.[60] Had the southern superintendent been given the same general cooperation which Loudoun accorded to Sir William Johnson, the story of Atkin's sojourn in office might have been somewhat different; but undoubtedly Loudoun recognized Atkin's limitations and hesitated to give him too much responsibility.

Despite his failings, Atkin was intelligent, well educated, and courageous. He was also a loyal servant of the Crown. An analysis of his writings reveals the fact that this Carolina merchant was familiar with the basic problems of Indian diplomacy and many of the difficulties in operating the office of imperial Indian superintendent. His detailed plans for periodic visitations, transportation of presents for his native wards, and classification of subordinates show a respectable knowledge concerning the obligations of his position.

One is driven to the conclusion that Atkin overwhelmed himself with plans and methods, giving far too much attention to detail. An example of his failing in this regard is found in his carefully planned, minute instructions for the ordering of Indian presents. His long memoranda include not only such ordinary articles as strouds, vermilion, blankets, and brass kettles, but also additional items like Indian paint boxes with separate compartments for different colored paints.[61] These boxes were to have mirrors inside the lids, and the outsides were to be decorated with birds, beasts, landscapes, forts, ships, and fruits. Another bequest which Atkin thoughtfully ordered for the Indians was a number of copper plates with a picture of George II leaning on a cannon on one side and a man-of-war under full sail on the other.

The superintendent's fascination with detail, however, is the very thing that gives him, today, a claim to historical recognition. His penchant for planning caused him to compose a scheme for imperial Indian control, the outstanding achievement of his lifetime. The document, remarkably preserved among the Loudoun papers in the Henry E. Huntington Library, is a copy of the original manuscript which Atkin presented to the Board of Trade on May 30, 1755. This copy has numerous notes and marginal captions by the superintendent. It is partly in his handwriting, and the report bears his signature as a true copy. The original has never been located, although a personal search was made by the writer in London in the Public Record Office and the British Museum in the summer of 1949. The Huntington Library document is bound in faded marble paper and comprises fifty-five

---

[60] An illustration can be found in the division of presents for the northern and southern Indians. William Johnson apparently persuaded Loudoun to give almost twice as much merchandise to the northern Indians, LO 2507.

[61] LO 3517. See also Atkin's long list of tools for resident blacksmiths living among the Indians, LO 3246.

folio pages of handwriting.[62] A discussion of the highlights of the document will be helpful in clarifying the main points of the report.

Atkin commences his essay by thanking the Lords of Trade for an opportunity of expressing his sentiments upon Indian affairs in general. He then goes on to point out that Indian affairs are, as he calls it, on a "wretched footing throughout all of America," and that some general plan of management is necessary before the Indians in disgust turn their allegiance entirely to the French. It is imperative, the essay further advises, that the English support and protect the Indians, since the tribesmen are the strongest barrier against French encroachment. Such regard for the Indians is extremely important, Atkin maintains, in view of the remarkable successes of the French in winning the friendship of key tribes among the nations which border the British provinces. Even the Cherokee and the Six Nations, Atkin complains, are turning away from the British.

Following his discourse upon the importance of Indians, Atkin then proceeds to analyze the reasons for French power among the native settlements west of the Appalachians. He notes that persons unfamiliar with Indian problems believe that the numerous French forts scattered throughout the Indian nations are responsible for the French strength.[63] Fortifications are not the source of French power, Atkin argues, because the Indians are not dominated by fear, but by friendship. Such small fortifications could be easily overwhelmed by the savage hordes that surround them. The Indians consider the French as benefactors, Atkin declares, because the warriors are continually supplied with ammunition, guns, and many other presents. Moreover, the French provide gunsmiths to sharpen native hatchets and to mend broken weapons. Atkin reasons that the French, with their understanding of the primitive mind, knew that a warrior would treasure a repaired weapon more than any new weapon which might be given to him, even as an outright present. Thus, Atkin points out, the French preserve the friendship of their Indian allies by the judicious use of presents and gunsmiths under the direction of a centralized Indian administration which tolerates no injustice to the Indian, even from the French traders.

Having perhaps unduly praised the French methods of Indian control, Atkin then launches into a critical discussion of Indian management and Indian commerce throughout all the British continental colonies. As one might expect, the chief target for his censures is South Carolina, his own province. What is true in South Carolina, Atkin argues, is true in some degree in all of the colonies. Generally speaking, he concludes that mismanagement

---

[62] LO 578.

[63] For a discussion of the French fortification system and French Indian policy, see Wilbur R. Jacobs, "Presents to Indians along the French Frontiers in the Old Northwest, 1748-63," *Indiana Magazine of History*, Vol. XLIV, No. 3 (September, 1948), pp. 245-56.

and chaos in Indian affairs will, in time, bring about alienation of all the Indian nations. In his own words, ". . . we neither build Forts for their Protection, nor mend their Guns and Hatchets for them, as they [the French] do . . . we set no Account by any of them, but [as] Hunters for the sake of Skins; And . . . our Traders Cheat and impose upon them." [64]

Edmond Atkin's main contention appears to be that every faction within the colonies that had anything to do with the Indians considered only its own private interests and not the general good of the government. The result was confusion, especially for the Indians, who did not know whom to believe when rival trading interests, for example, did not hesitate to tell the boldest lies about each other.

Although Atkin deplored the lack of unity within the colonies respecting Indian policy, he had some even warmer words for the rum traders who caused, what he terms, "scandal," "alarm," and "uneasiness" in their contemptible dealings. Atkin is not alone in this opinion. Most administrators in the colonies shared his views concerning the traders.[65]

One of the most valuable parts of Atkin's whole essay is the section which he terms the "Character of the Indians." Here is found a long discussion on each of the major Indian confederacies which bordered the British colonies from Massachusetts to Georgia. Because of his deep insight into the psychology of the Indian, his introductory statements might well have been written by Sir William Johnson, or, at a later date, by Francis Parkman.

> No people in the World understand and pursue their true National Interest, better than the Indians. How sanguinary soever they are towards their Enemies, from a misguided Passion of Heroism, and a love of their country; yet they are otherways truly humane, hospitable, and equitable. And how fraudulent soever they have been reputed, from the Appearance of their military Actions, in which according to their method of War, Glory cannot be accquired without Cunning and Stratagem; Yet in their publick Treaties no People on earth are more open, explicit, and Direct. Nor are they excelled by any in the observance of them.[66]

Following this beginning, the essay widens into a geographical and historical description of the major tribes surrounding the British provinces. Because particular emphasis is placed upon the southern "nations," one finds similarities between this work and James Adair's memorable *History of the American Indians*, published in 1775. Certainly Atkin's presentation compares favorably with that of Adair on several counts. In terms of clear reasoning

---

[64] LO 578, pp. 20-21 (p. 37, below).

[65] Robert Dinwiddie, lieutenant governor of Virginia, referred to the traders as "abandoned wretches."

[66] LO 578, p. 21 (p. 38, below).

and general accuracy of information Atkin seems to score a point. He appears, for the most part, to have lost the vindictive attitude toward his contemporaries which characterized his footnoted memoir on the Choctaw revolt. By contrast, Adair's *History* is colored by glaring prejudices and personal hatreds. This is not to say that Atkin's essay could ever replace Adair's notable *History*. Rather the two writings complement each other in illuminating an era of no little obscurity. Atkin's work, which antedates Adair's by twenty years, offers another approach to Indian problems. Both are significant documentary accounts of the southern Indians and southern history. Other distinguishing features of Atkin's essay are that locations of forts and Indian towns are given, and a long enumeration of warrior strength is compiled. His figures regarding Indian fighting men closely tally with estimates by Governor James Glen of South Carolina, by John Stuart, Atkin's successor, and by William Johnson.[67]

Close examination of Atkin's writing indicates that he had extensive notes, government documents, statutes, and copies of the records of the South Carolina Council and Assembly at his disposal. Checking of his quotations shows them to be reasonably accurate and not distorted.[68] One note of caution should be observed, however. Atkin had his own purposes in mind in writing the report and occasionally has played up Indian virtues so as to show what he could do if he were appointed superintendent. This is apparent in his account of the outbreak of the Yamasee War of 1715-1716. Verner Crane's account of the war, in *The Southern Frontier, 1670-1732*, shows Atkin to be incomplete but not in error.

The last section of the essay is devoted entirely to the future superintendent's scheme for a general overhauling of existing Indian administration in North America. The objectives of his plan are to correct the evils of maladministration which he outlined in the first part of the manuscript. Indian alliances were to be revived, and a uniform regulation of Indian commerce was to be put into effect. These measures would help to defeat what Atkin terms "the designs of the French."

At this point Atkin plunges into a detailed description of his proposed design for Indian administration, which, because of its magnitude, can be but briefly sketched here. The focal point of his plan is the appointment of two imperial superintendents with full parliamentary authority and proper financial backing to carry out their duties. The northern superintendent was

---

[67] Chapman J. Milling (ed.), *Colonial South Carolina: Two Contemporary Descriptions* (Columbia, S. C., 1951), has estimates by Glen. Stuart's report is in "Total number of Gun Men in the Southern District," December 1, 1764, an unidentified Public Record Office transcript on file at the Illinois Historical Survey, University of Illinois. Johnson's enumerations are in *New York Colonial Documents*, VII, 582-84.

[68] Atkin's quotations from the Indian trading act of 1752 have only minor changes. The act is found in Thomas Cooper (ed.), *The Statutes at Large of South Carolina* (Columbia, S.C., 1838), III, 763 ff.

to have jurisdiction over the Iroquoian confederacy and its allies, and the southern counterpart was to govern British relations with the southern tribes, the Cherokee, and their Muskhogean brothers.

One of the first duties of the superintendents was to be the negotiation of a series of treaties with all the principal Indian nations which would bind the tribesmen to British trade and to British friendship. The Indians were to agree to trade only with the English, and new trade regulations were to be established by law in order to protect the natives from abuses. Atkin declares that Indian commerce had to follow a regular procedure with licensed traders, fixed prices, and standard weights and measures. In addition, strict penalties were to be directed against any trader who allowed Indians to become drunk. Spirits given to the warriors had to be "temper'd" with water.

Atkin's scheme further provided for an extensive system of forts and block-houses to be erected by British army engineers. The purpose of these forts was to "protect" the Indians from the French, to provide a storing place for presents and goods for Indian commerce, and to garrison soldiers. One can see that the future superintendent was advocating a duplication of the French system of fortifications where government agents, licensed traders, and interpreters, in Atkin's opinion, had the only direct contact with the Indians.[69] Atkin cautions at this point that private individuals should have no contact with the Indians, especially in connection with land purchases. All Indian affairs were to be under the general direction of the superintendent.

The list of assistants for the superintendent, enumerated by Atkin, shows that he overlooked no possibility of acquiring help. Among those mentioned are S.P.G. missionaries,[70] frontier rangers, secretaries, gunsmiths, interpreters, and commissioners. All these helpers were needed, Atkin maintains, to aid the superintendent in distributing presents and in making frequent visitations among his Indian wards.

Such a program of Indian administration as has been briefly outlined here would obviously be of tremendous expense to the imperial government. Atkin was not oblivious to the cost of putting his scheme into operation; he declares that the colonies should provide part of the funds and suggests three methods of raising revenue. The first was a poll tax to be levied upon every provincial male subject. Should Parliament, however, be reluctant to impose this tax, Atkin thoughtfully put forth the alternative of a "small" duty upon wines imported from the West Indies and an "easy" duty upon *"forreign* Sugars, Melasses & Rum." His third suggestion was the establishment of a system of

---

[69] Francis Parkman has pointed out the many irregularities and instances of illegal trade in New France. See, for example, *Count Frontenac and New France under Louis XIV* (Boston, 1893), pp. 26-43.

[70] For a scholarly account of the work of the Society of the Propagation of the Gospel in Foreign Parts, see Frank J. Klingberg, *Anglican Humanitarianism in Colonial New York* (Philadelphia, 1940).

post offices throughout all of North America, which he believed would "under good regulations bring in a large sum."

Edmond Atkin's plan for imperial control of the Indians was not responsible for setting up the Indian superintendency system, but it was truly the first comprehensive, well-organized design for Indian management submitted to British authorities. The basic ideas were not new to the Board of Trade, but the details of Atkin's scheme reflected his long experience as a merchant in dealing with the Indian trade and his familarity with Indian problems as a member of the South Carolina Council for some seventeen years.[71] Professor C. H. McIlwain, in his introduction to *Wraxall's Abridgement* of Indian Affairs, suggested that Peter Wraxall's work was responsible for the creation of the office of Indian superintendent.[72] Wraxall's influence seems to be over-rated by McIlwain, however, and Professor John Richard Alden maintains, in a later article in the *Mississippi Valley Historical Review*,[73] that the deliberations of the Albany conference of 1754 were primarily responsible for creating the Indian superintendency offices. Alden points out that the recommendations of William Johnson and of the colonial statesman Thomas Pownall were enclosed with the Albany conference journals when they were sent to the Board of Trade.[74] It should be noted, nevertheless, that these recommendations were preceded by a publication of a member of the New York Council, Archibald Kennedy, who suggested the office of superintendent as early as 1751.[75] It is known that Kennedy's pamphlet inspired Cadwallader Colden in 1751 to write a report on Indian affairs which reached the Board of Trade.[76] Thomas Pownall was also familiar with Kennedy's work.[77]

Regardless of these writings, it is certain that Atkin's design for Indian management was the earliest scheme that worked all previous ideas of Indian administration into one coherent plan. Above all, the distinguishing achievement of Edmond Atkin was, in the words of the late John Carl Parish, that

---

[71] Verner Crane identifies the firm of "Atkins" in connection with the Indian trade in the late 1730's. See his *Southern Frontier*, p. 121, n. 54. Atkin had been on the Council since 1738.

[72] Charles Howard McIlwain (ed.), *An Abridgement of the Indian Affairs . . . Transacted in the Colony of New York, from the Year 1678 to the Year 1751* (Cambridge, Mass., 1915), pp. xcvii-c.

[73] "The Albany Congress and the Creation of the Indian Superintendencies," Vol. XXVII, No. 2 (September, 1940), pp. 193-210.

[74] *Ibid.*

[75] Archibald Kennedy, *The Importance of Gaining and Preserving the Friendship of the Indians to the British Interest Considered* (New York, 1751), pp. 7 ff.

[76] Alden, "The Albany Congress and the Creation of the Indian Superintendencies," *loc. cit.*

[77] John A. Schutz, *Thomas Pownall, British Defender of American Liberty . . .* (Glendale, Calif., 1951), p. 41.

of writing a "historical narrative and description of the southern Indians . . . unequaled in his time."[78] Atkin's report and especially his plan are further distinguished as illustrations of the kind of mercantile policy that was to be a prelude to the American Revolution.[79]

---

[78] Parish, *The Persistence of the Westward Movement*, p. 160. Meriwether, *Expansion of South Carolina*, contains a scholarly account of the advance of the frontier during the period covered by Atkin's report. See pp. 117 ff.

[79] See LO 578 (pp. 93 ff., below).

Bibliographical Note on Unpublished Materials

The most important body of manuscript concerning Edmond Atkin's career is in the Henry E. Huntington Library collection of Loudoun Papers. Here is found his report and the plan for imperial Indian control of 1755. Atkin's correspondence with the Earl of Loudoun, with colonial governors, military officials, and assistants is included in this large collection. The Loudoun Papers are particularly rich in connection with the superintendent's work in Virginia. This collection is supplemented by Atkin documents in the Abercromby Papers, although there is some duplication of materials. The Huntington Manuscripts, a third collection, also contain a few items concerning Atkin.

Among the materials in the Public Record Office in London, many of the Colonial Office Papers and War Office Papers have proved valuable. Class 5, Volumes 50, 64, and 374, mainly covering military correspondence and Indian affairs, has yielded much biographical data regarding Atkin; and Classes 323 and 324 also include items on the superintendent. In the War Office Papers, Class 34, the Amherst Papers, Volume 47 (letters from officials in South Carolina and Virginia to the commander-in-chief), are letters relating to the later period of Atkin's work as superintendent.

Among the Lansdowne Papers in the British Museum is Atkin's elaborate memoir on the Choctaw revolt. The Additional Manuscripts volumes contain an item which gives a complete accounting of Atkin's expenses in connection with his official duties.

Transcriptions of a number of the above documents are available in the Library of Congress, the Public Archives of Canada, the Illinois Historical Survey, Urbana, Illinois, and the Louis Knott Koontz Collection at the University of California at Los Angeles. The Bouquet Papers in the Public Archives of Canada are useful in the study of the Indian frontier during the late 1750's and early 1760's.

At the Historical Commission of South Carolina is an abundance of material relating to the southern Indian frontier. The Council House Journals from 1738 to 1760 cover Atkin's work in the upper house; and the Journals of the Commons House of Assembly include more useful information, especially in regard to his committee work and relations with members of the lower house. Fortunately the Journals of the Commons House of Assembly are now being edited by the Director of the Historical Commission, Dr. J. H. Easterby, and the edited material covering the period 1736-1742 was used in preference to the original manuscript. Although the name of the superintendent appears only infrequently in the "Indian Books of South Carolina," these six bound volumes are an invaluable source of information regarding the Indian frontier of the southern colonies. Volume I, a journal of the Indian commissioners, has been published in part, under the editorship of A. S. Salley, as *Journal of the Commissioners of the Indian Trade of South Carolina, September 20, 1710—April 12, 1715* (Columbia, S.C., 1926); Volumes II to VI, covering the period, 1749-1760, are chiefly letter books, recorded by the clerk of the council. There is evidence that the Indian books covering the period of the 1740's were lost. ("Council Journals," Volume XVII [1748-1749], p. 428). The Historical Commission also has several records of land purchases along the Pee Dee River by Edmond and John Atkin.

MAPS

Two contemporary maps have been of special value. "A Map of the British and French Dominions in North America . . ." by John Mitchell (London 1755), William L. Clements Library, Ann Arbor, Michigan, is the most accurate and complete of the maps made in the 1750's. Eman Bowen's "An Accurate Map of North America . . ." (London [1763]) has less detailed information but is reliable within limitations of geographical knowledge of the times. An original copy of the Bowen map is in the John Carter Brown Library, Providence, Rhode Island.

A third map which has been used, "Map of the Southern Indian District of North America Compiled under the Direction of John Stuart," by Joseph Purcell [1773], Edward E. Ayer Collection, Newberry Library, Chicago, Illinois, is a cumbersome work in which the symbols for Indian towns and forts are not easily ascertained. Henry Mouzon's "An Accurate Map of North and South Carolina with their Indian Frontiers . . ." (London, 1776), Historical Commission of South Carolina, is useful for the study of Carolina trading paths to the frontier.

THE EDMOND ATKIN REPORT OF 1755

Editorial Note

Edmond Atkin was not writing a book for publication in 1755, and for this reason the reader should exercise moderate tolerance in examining his work. Except for the lowering of superior letters, eighteenth-century spelling and misspelling, inconsistency in spelling, capitalization, and punctuation have been transferred from the written manuscript to the printed page without any alteration. The transcribed document has been carefully collated with the original manuscript and the reader may assume that the printed words are as Atkin or his scribe wrote them.

The document here reproduced, by permission of The Huntington Library, San Marino, California, is a copy, made by a scribe, of an undiscovered original by Atkin. It is obvious, however, that Atkin read this copy carefully, for all the marginal notes are made in his handwriting. He also corrected the scribe's copying. These corrections by Atkin are indicated in the pages that follow by enclosure in fancy brackets—**[]**—roman type indicating additions, and italic type indicating deletions. Ordinary brackets—[]—except for a few occasions duly pointed out in the footnotes, indicate insertions made by the editor. Bracketed numbers—[2]—mark the beginning of new pages of the manuscript.

Copy

To the Right Honourable, the Lords Commissioners for Trade and Plantations

N:B
This is a Copy of a Letter penned in 1754 by desire of the Board of Trade and lodged in the hands of the Earl of Halifax 30 May 1755 Edm.d Atkin

My Lords

When you did me the Honour to require mine to lay before you in writing my Sentiments upon the Indian Affairs in general in North America, it gave me a Pleasure; Because it made me entertain some Hope, that the close Attention I paid to their Affairs, the Care I bestow'd to inform, and the Service done I made upon them, for many Years since His Majesty honoured me in 1738 with a Seat in his Council for the Province of South Carolina, might prove at last not altogether useless.

As I remember right I told your Lordships, That the whole System of our Indian Affairs was a wretched Scything throughout all America; That unless the Direction and Management of them respectively altered, and brought under some General Plan, it was impossible but that our Interest among the Indian Nations now in Alliance with us must continue to decline, as it had done of late Years, until we should lose them very soon; And that I thought it was yet in our Power, not only to retrieve what we had lost to the French, but firmly to establish the future Security and Welfare of our Colonies on the Continent. I endeavour to make your Lordships acquainted with some Facts as proofs, performing a National Justice. Offices, to found all the common Practice, And the same I apprehend desire to labour for, in case time, the same great Quickening in his highest Breaking, would say, That nature alone might be effectually surrendered to Examination.

The Importance of Indians is now generally known and understood. Doubt remains not but the Prosperity of our Colonies on the Continent, will stand or falls with our Interest and favour among them. While they are our Friends they are the Cheapest and strongest Barrier for the Protection of our Settlements; when Enemies, they are capable of ravaging in their method of War in spite of all we can do, to render them, if we consider almost useless. If this the French see as possible, is well of their Natural. And we must see how and their meer that they have employed all their Art; not only to embroil us with our Indians, and to set it work clandestinely some of their own to massacre our People even in times of Peace; but to destroy and wholly extirpate those Nations whose Affections they could not gain, by setting one against another, and themselves pretending to do it. The same Reason should certainly make it our Policy to support and Preserve them.

Since the French opened and established some Years ago a shorter Communication between Canada and Louisiana, by way of the River Wabash, instead of the Illinois River, into the Mississippi, they have bent all their Endeavours to the making themselves. Masters also of the River Ohio, the Hoghoge or great Cherokee River and other Rivers that run from the Eastward into the same; and to the advancing upon, & confining our Possessions within the Heads of the Rivers that run into the Atlantick Ocean. From the Year 1745 during the late War, they have been particularly active and Diligent in courting and Treating those of the Six united Nations and other Indians who live upon the Waters of the Ohio, on the back of Pensilvania, Maryland, and Virginia; and with the Cherokees

---

THE FIRST PAGE OF ATKIN'S REPORT OF 1755

(Courtesy Huntington Library)

[N.B.

This is a Copy of a Letter penned in 1754 by desire of the Board of Trade and lodged in the hands of the Earl of Halifax 30 May 1755.[1]

EDMD ATKIN]

MY LORDS

When you did me the Honour to require me to lay before your Lordships, my Sentiments upon the Indian Affairs in general in North America, it gave me a Pleasure; Because it made me entertain some Hope, that the close Attention I paid to those Affairs, the Time I devoted to them, and the observations I made upon them for many Years since his Majesty honourd me in 1738 with a Seat in his Council for the province of South Carolina, might prove at last not altogether useless.

If I remember right I told your Lordships, That the whole System of our Indian Affairs was on a wretched footing throughout all America, That unless the Direction and Management of them was intirely alter'd and brought under some General Plan, it was impossible but that our Interest among the Indian Nations now in Alliance with us, must continue to decline as it had done of late Years, until [*that*] we should have scarce any left; And that I thought it was yet in our Power, not only to retreive what we had lost to the French but firmly to establish the future Security and Welfare of our Colonies on the Continent. I undertook to make your Lordships acquainted with some Facts, necessary for forming a Judgment on those Affairs; to point out the Errors in practice; the Measures I apprehended proper to be taken for remydying the Same, and for attaining our proper objects; as well as after what manner they might be effectually carried into Execution.

Intent of these Sheets

The Importance of Indians is now generally known and understood. a Doubt remains not, that the prosperity of our Colonies on the Continent, will stand or fall with our Interest and favour among them. While they are our Friends, they are the Cheapest and strongest Barrier for the Protection of our Settlements; when

Importance of Indians

---

[1] Wide powers were delegated to the Board of Trade, one of the most important of which was to supervise the administration of the colonies. George Montagu Dunk, 2d Earl of Halifax, was president of the Board of Trade from 1748 to 1761.

Enemies, they are capable by ravaging in their method of War, in spite of all we can do, to render those Possessions almost useless. Of this the French are so sensible, as well as of our Natural Advantages beyond their own, that they have employed all their Art, not only to embroil us with our Indians, and to Set at work clandestinely some of their own to scalp our People even in times of Peace, but to destroy and utterly extirpate those Nations whose Affections they coud not gain, by setting one against another, and themselves assisting to do it.[2] The same Reason should certainly make it our Policy, to support and preserve them.

Designs &
Operations of
the French

Since the French open'd and establish'd some Years ago a shorter [cC]ommunication between Canada and Louisiana by way of the River Wabash, instead of the Illinois River, into the Missisipi, they have bent all their Measures to the making themselves Masters also of the River Ohio, the Hogohege or great Cherokee River,[3] and other Rivers that run from the Eastward into the Same; and to the advancing upon, & confining our Posessions, within the Heads of the Rivers that run into the Atlantick Ocean— From the Year 1745 during the late War, they have been particularly active and Diligent in courting and Treating with those of the Six united Nations and other Indians who live upon the Waters of the Ohio,[4] on the back of Pensilvania, Maryland, and Virginia; and with the [2] Cherokees on the back of Carolina, to obtain leave to build Forts among them. They then met with a favourable Reception on the Ohio, and did take some small footing on the back of Pensilvania, at or near one of the Heads of that River, on the South side of Lake Erie; tho it was not attended to, nor seems to have been generally known. Poudret[5] and Limnate, who were at [that]

---

[2] This policy was used by the French against the Chickasaw. See *Adair's History*, pp. 380 ff. For the French policy in the North, see *New York Colonial Documents*, X, 295-96.

[3] Or the Tennessee River. See Donald Davidson, *The Tennessee* . . . (New York, 1946), I, 38-39; "A Map of the British and French Dominions in North America . . ." by John Mitchell (London, 1755); "An Accurate Map of North America . . ." by Eman Bowen (London, [1763]). A copy of the Mitchell map is in the William L. Clements Library, and an original of the Bowen map is in the John Carter Brown Library.

[4] Iroquois on the Ohio were called Mingoes. The total number of warriors living in the Ohio area in 1748 was estimated at 789. See *Minutes of the Provincial Council of Pennsylvania*, V, 351.

[5] Atkin possibly refers to one Vincent Poudret who was employed by the governor of Canada as a messenger in 1740. *Collections* of the State

time and on that occasion employd by the Governors of Canada and Louisiana, to carry Presents to all our Indians South of the Lakes, and invite them to a general Treaty of Peace with the French, and to stir them up by the prospect of great Booty, to fall upon the back settlements of Virginia and Carolina, were heard to say by some English Prisoners taken on Aligany River, "That the Indians throughout America would soon be their Friends; that they would carry all smooth with the Indians, till by presents they had got Permission to build Forts among their Towns, and then would care little for them or the English, for that it it would never be in the Power of either to demolish them." Some of the lower Cherokees were at the same time greatly corrupted by the help of two of their Head men that were in England in 1730,[6] who return'd as Emissaries from Canada, where they had been carried Prisoners, and lived some Years, being there made very much of: All the Indian Nations in Friendship with Carolina, being at that Juncture dissatisfied, concerted a Rupture with us; except the Catawbas, who alone refused to consent thereto, and discover'd it to us. And several Steps towards it were taken, and many Outrages committed within the settlements of that Province. The upper Cherokees having agreed to a Peace with the French and other Indians, permitted the French Colours to be set up in one of their Towns beyond the Mountains. And not long before to wit in 1744, it appeared by a Letter from Monsr. Vaudreuil Governor of Louisiana to the Count de Maurepas the French Secretary of State, which was intercepted, "That he proposed from the French Fort[7] at the Alibamaes in the upper Creek Nation, situated on the River that falls into the Bay of Mobile, to penetrate Eastward so far as into the Lower Creek Nation upon the Chattahuchee River, (which taken it's rise among some of the lower Cherokee Towns, at the foot of the Mountains, runs into

---

Historical Society of Wisconsin, ed. R. G. Thwaites (Madison, 1906), XVII, 331.

[6] For a scholarly account of the famous Cherokee embassy of 1730, see Crane, *Southern Frontier*, pp. 276-80, 295-302. Attakullakulla, or Little Carpenter, was one of the chiefs captured by the French. See Alden, *John Stuart*, p. 33. This chief was suspected of having French sympathies. See Raymond Demeré to ———, Bouquet Papers, Public Archives of Canada, A. 13, pp. 76-79.

[7] Fort Alabama, or Fort Toulouse, was built near the confluence of the Coosa and the Tallapoosa rivers. Atkin writes that it was constructed in 1715. See LO 578, p. 6 (p. 11, below). Crane, *Southern Frontier*, 256 n., states it was built in 1717 but indicates much confusion in contemporary records concerning the date.

the Bay of Apalatchee in the Gulf of Mexico). And he thought he might succeed in driving out the English, who had Magazines in all those parts". Accordingly in 1750, Malatchi [8] Chief of the lower Creeks being induced to invite some of the French from the said Fort to his Town Coweta,[9] two or three Officers (of whom one was an Engineer), and some private Men did then go, were kindly received, and permitted to set up the French Colours in that Town; while the request of some of our Traders to set up our Colours was disregarded.

Consequences
of their
Succeeding.

From this View of the late Operations and designs of the French to the South of the Lakes, it readily appears, that if they succeed therein intirely, the hitherto imaginary Boundary Line, which they have set in some of their Maps to all our Colonies on their backs Westward, will be in Fact realiz'd by a Chain of Posts in Posession. Then, according to their own and our Colony Management of Indian Affairs, they must soon exclude us totally from the before-mention'd and other Western Nations, with whom we at present carry on a very considerable Branch of Commerce. For altho tis impossible for them to introduce their own Goods from New Orleans on Missisippi River, to the Northward; or from Montreal on the River at St. Lawrence, [3] to the Southward, so far to the Back of our Settlements, on any reasonable Terms; yet they will not fail of getting sufficient Supplies of Goods fit for the Indians, and that better and Cheaper than their own, directly from the Atlantick Ocean through our Colonies, by means of British Subjects therein; As they have had heretofore at Montreal in Canada; from the Merchants of New York.[10] And they will have it in their Power in any Future War, more especially from a Fort built in one of the upper Cherokee Towns (which being in a Central Place may be supported alike or equally from Montreal, or New Orleans, the Ilinois, and other intermediate Posts, almost every foot of the way by Water; and at the same time, being on the other side of the Mountains, cannot be attacked by us without great Forces and great Expense) not only by means of the

---

[8] Malatchi, chief headman of the Lower Creeks was the son of a famous chief called "Old Emperor Brim." See Meriwether, *Expansion of South Carolina*, p. 205. Frequent references to the son are found in "Indian Books of South Carolina," Vol. V. For example, see pp. 7, 29, 100.

[9] Coweta was an old Creek town located near present Columbus, Georgia. Crane, *Southern Frontier*, p. 134 n.

[10] The history of the illegal trade between Canada and New York is summarized in *New York Colonial Documents*, VII, 16.

7

Indians to harrass and break up the back Settlements of our Southern Colonies, but easily to invade either of them in due form, and gain a Port on the Atlantick Ocean, which it is our invariable Maxim by all means possible to prevent. I wave saying any thing in particular of the like Steps taken by the French in pursuit of the same object on the Back of New York, New England and Nova Scotia; because I suppose them to be much better known to your Lordships. I only beg leave to observe, That the Measures pursued are uniformly the same, from the Mouth of St. Lawrance River, to that of Missippi; And that the French have made a much greater impression, and gain'd more upon the Six United Nations, their Dependents, and other Indians contiguous to those Northern Colonies, than they have yet done upon the Cherokees, or any of the Southern Nations hitherto wholly dependent on Carolina. For the Six Nations altogether, have a long time past shewn manifestly a disposition to act a Neutral part between us and the French; Some of them have actually taken part with, and assisted the French privately. And the Government of New York hath at times acknowledged a Jealousy of their total Disaffection.

Having taken this short view of the Posture of Indian Affairs, between our own and the French Colonies, it is worth while to consider, whence it comes to Pass that, possess'd as we are of vastly superior Advantages, by Situation on the Ocean, by our Conveniencies for the quick and easy introduction of our Goods to the Inland Parts, by the Quality and Cheapness of our Goods fit for Indians, and by the natural disposition of the Indians to prefer us, from a greater similarity between their and our Government, the French have notwithstanding, in spite of their own very great disadvantages in all those Respects, made so rapid a Progress even among Nations nearest to our Settlements, as hath lately surprized every Body. It is universally known, that the Indian [affairs] have been managed and conducted on one general plan, steadily pursued througout Canada and Louisiana, under the immediate direction of the Crown; the chief object of which is, to exclude us not only from the Missisipi but from all the Indian Nations on this side of it. In the execution whereof are employed Men of the greatest Knowledge and Experience, by early and long Service, from among the Officers, and Missionaries; who are supported out of the Trade with the Indians, who rest their hopes of Preferment on their own Behaviour, and who on all Occasions support the Honour and Dignity of the French Nation, and watch all opportunities to turn every Occurrence to their own Advantage, or to the Disadvantage of great Britain and her Colonies. And in every Nation where the[y] can obtain the least opening for it, they fail not either by Consent or Compulsion, to place Forts and Garrisons howsoever small, under pretence of protecting those Indians against their Enemies, (which are sometimes of their own Creating for the Purpose), but with a real Intention to establish a Claim of Posession, and to fix Boundaries to us. Whereas on the other hand, the Conduct of our Colonies hath been as various as their different Interests, arising from their different Situations, which have been the [4] Foundation of as many distinct local and partial Considerations. Without a mutual regard for the Interest of the whole, some of them relying for their Security and the Continuance of a friendly Commerce with the Indians, on its own Importance to them, have not extended their Care even to their own Frontiers, but have confined their object only to the keeping mischief from their doors. The French have accordingly taught the Indians to consider our Colonies, as so many separate independent Communities, having no Concern with each other. Whence it hath arisen that the Indians in Peace and Amity with one of them, have at the same time behaved as enemies towards the people of another. Some of the Colonies have made no regulations at all in the Indian Affairs; others have made different ones, and some but seldom if at all sent proper Persons to look into them. But the management of them hath often been left to Traders, who have no Skill in Public Affairs, are directed only by their own Interest, and being generally the loosest kind of People, are despis'd and held in great Contempt by the Indians as Liars, and Persons regarding nothing but their own Gain.[11] All those things are pretty well known.

As it is commonly supposed, that the French have acquired their influence, and maintain their Power among the Indian Nations, intirely by their Forts; —it seems also to have been generally thought, that if they are not [to] be removed, yet our Building Forts in the same Places, and in such other places where the French still propose to do it, will be a Sufficient remedy to put an intire stop to the same, and to secure our own Interest. But this will be found on a more intimate accquaintance

---

[11] Adair believed that "discreet orderly traders" were of great benefit to the colonies. He had, however, no sympathy for the "Arab-like pedlars" who cheated the Indians and "injured" the other traders. *Adair's History*, pp. 394 ff.

with that subject, to be a very great Error. How usefull and necessary soever Forts really are, for establishing between the Crowns of Great Britain and France marks of Possession, or for the mutual protection of their Traders and Friends, and for fixing the doubtfull and wavering among the Indians; yet it is truly a great absurdity to imagine, that either the French or ourselves can maintain an Interest & Influence, more especially among the Inland Nations, barely by the Possession of Forts, without being at the same time possess'd of their *Affections;* Or that anything less than such a Wall as is built between China and Tartary can, when the Indians are our Enemies, secure our wide extended and exposed Colonies from their Incursions. Most of the French inland Forts are small, and very weak, having but few Men. And tho' the Indians are unskilled, and unprovided for the Attack of Forts, yet the Garrisons of the largest may easily be starv'd by them into a Surrender whenever they please. We must [look] therefore into the Conduct and Management of the French in those Forts, in order to discover by the *Arts* practiced therein the true causes from whence, under a Commerce clogged with a most hazardous Navigation & expensive Transportation of Goods, with the additional load of paying all the Charges of their Government, and under a total inability at any rate of supplying all the wants of the Indians, they have still gain'd their Affections, and consequently that surprising Influence which we have felt. Those Arts will be found to be the most Simple, the most easy and certain, and the least expensive imaginable. The two Principal ones are, the Provision of *Gunsmiths,* and not so much valuable Presents as a judicious Application of them.[12] We furnish the Indians with Guns enough in exchange for their deer skins and Furrs; but the French mend them and keep them in repair Gratis. We are sometimes almost lavish of presents on particular Occasions, which in the way they are given produce but little good Effect with those that receive them, and still less with their Nation. But the French by a constant prudent Practice, make even Trifles productive of the most desirable National Consequences. When an Indian after undergoing the mortification of having a Gun (perhaps from trial and use become a favourite one) suddenly by some slight

---

[12] Accounts of French presents for Indians are found in *The Present State of the Country . . . of Louisiana.* By an Officer at New Orleans . . . (London, 1744), pp. 53 ff.; Vaudreuil Letter Book, 1744, LO 26.

accident to the Lock, or Touch hole, render'd intirely useless to him, I say when he sees it afterwards as suddenly restored to [5] its former State, and as usefull as before, it gladdens his Heart more than a present of a new Gun would. He then looks on our Trader and the Frenchman with different Eyes. The former only Sold him the Gun (perhaps at an extravagant price); the latter when it is spoiled, hath as it were new made [it] for nothing. This endears the Frenchman to him. He is glad to have such a Friend near him. Their mutual Convenience unites them. Gratitude inclines the Indian to oblige him by any means in his Power. The presents to Indians are made at the expence of the Crown of France. Besides those given by the Governors at periodical Meetings, some are left in the occasional disposition of the Commanders of Forts the Year round. A present of any Value is never given by them but to an Indian of Sway and Consequence [among the Warriours], or as an Orator among the people. And then he comes by it easy, and without any Trouble. Whereas when such do receive Presents of some Value from us, they earn them much too dearly by tiresome tedious Journies of some hundred Miles, and the loss of time from their Hunts, which they know would have turn'd to better Account. Even trifles are put on the footing of things of Value at the French Forts, by bestowing them chiefly on the old Head Men of Note, who being past the fatigue of War and constant Hunting for their Livelyhood, but on Account of their Age held in great Veneration for their Wisdom and Experience, spend the remainder of their days almost intirely in the Town Round Houses, where the Youth and others daily report; relating to them the History of their Nation, discoursing of Occurrences, and delivering precepts and Instructions for their Conduct and Welfare. Which is all the Indian Education. To these old men who are unable to purchase Necessaries, or to perform long Journeys, when they visit those Forts the French give from time to time a Load or two of Powder and Ball, a Flint, a Knife, a little Paint, a flap or shirt, and the like. The Old Men repay the French largely for those Trifles, in their Harrangues at the round Houses, by great Encomiums on their kindness, and recommendations of them to favour; which often inculcated, make impressions on the Youth, that grow up with them into a confirm'd prejudice. On the other hand those old men complain, that our Traders, who confine their kindness and Civility almost wholly to the Young Hunters for the sake of their deerskins, shew Slights to them which lessen them in the Eyes of their People. The vast Quantity of Ammunition with which the French furnish the Indians every where by their Water Carriage more Conveniently than we can, hath strengthened their influence, that Article being the only means the Indians have to get everything else they stand in need of. Ammunition, especially Bulletts, being heavy and a Horse Load but of small Value, our Traders who are oblig'd to carry on their Trade in the Southern Parts, where the most numerous Indians are, many hundred Miles wholly by Horse Carriage, naturally consulting their own greatest profitt, have carried but scanty supplies of that Article, and in a great measure left it to the French; who have thereby imperceptably accquir'd an Addition to their Interest, in a manner which hath hitherto pass'd almost unnotic'd; But is of so much consequence to them, that the Governour of new Orleans in a letter to the French Secretary of State, (which being intercepted in the late War is now in my hands)[13] gave it as his opinion, "That were it not for those great supplies of Ammunition, some Nations of Indians devoted to the English, would not suffer Frenchmen to remain among them. And therefore he propos'd even to restrain the Quantity, to make them more Submissive". The same reason should lead us by some means or other to encrease it.

The National Effects which the Skillfull application of little [presents] to particular Indians, and the providing Gunsmiths to mend the Guns of all in General hath produced, are scarce to be conceiv'd. The French in many places have made those two things alone as practices in their Forts, in conjunction with a better supply of Ammunition than our Traders carry, [6] almost counterballance every other disadvantage they labour under. To illustrate fully the truth of this observation, because I think it of moment, I make choice of the Alabama Fort in the upper Creek Nation, on the Mobile River.[14] That Fort being about 460 miles by Land from Charles Town, and about 300 miles by Water from Mobile, was built immediately upon the breaking out of the Indian War with Carolina in 1715, when that Province had Traders in every Town in the Nation, and was posess'd of the whole Indian Trade with the more Western

---

[13] Extracts of these captured messages appear in the Loudoun Papers. For example, LO 26 is Vaudreuil's letter book which relates to his governorship in Louisiana.

[14] Or Fort Toulouse. See note 7.

Nations, the Chicasaws, Chactaws, Natchees, and others, to the [very] Banks of the Missisippi River, near 900 miles back. At that time the foundations of New Orleans were not laid; and but three Years before there were but 28 French Families Settled in all that was calld Louisiana. Ever since the peace which was made with the Indians in general in 1718, [our Traders] have resided as before in all the Creek Towns, and supplied them plentifully with all goods, except Ammunition. The French have never been able to supply the Goods necessary for them, except that Article. Insomuch that the Governor of Louisiana, in another Letter in 1744 to the French Secretary of State acknowledged, "That the Indians upbraided them therewith, and their breach of promises on that Head." They have constantly been obliged to draw all their Necessaries for that Garrison from the Indians; and during the late War, were under the Necessity of purchasing from our Traders the very presents they gave them. And yet at that time, those Creek Indian Chiefs being earnestly press'd to it in Charles Town by the So. Carolina Government, refused not only to assist us in attacking that Albama Fort, but even to stand neuter while we did it ourselves; and could only be prevailed on to give their Consent, that we might build a Fort also in their Nation. At their return home, intelligence was given immediately to the Commander of the Albama Fort, of our Intention; and the whole Nation kept under alarm a long time, by the War whoop sent from Town to Town. Such sort of Attachments to the French have surprised most people. But their true Springs are really those I have given.

It is no small addit[t]ion to the influence of the French, that their Officers allways on the spot, both prevent Abuses being offer'd to the Indians by particular Persons, and also never fail to demand immediate Satisfaction for any Injuries or Insults offer'd by them; which is the more readily complied with. Whereas we not being in the like Condition to demand such Satisfaction for any offences, are obliged to put up with them, and are therefore slighted— None dare to talk with the Indians about State Affairs but standing Sworn Interpreters, and they only what is given in Charge; who occasionally throw out what is suitable for their Purposes. Whereas our Traders uncontrouled tell them every man what Story he pleases— I have nothing to add under this head but what all the World knows, the great share the French Missionaries have in influencing the Indians, by means of their Superstition;[15] whose service is such, that they have been esteemed almost of as much Consequence as Garrisons. They have been the means of gaining as much respect from the Indians to the French, as our Traders have caused disrespect to us, by their disolute Lives and Manners. And by accquiring their Confidence and Esteem, they have been able to penetrate the Thoughts and Designs of the Indians, when others could not; and when they could do no more, have at least given time to the Governors to take measures for disconcerting their Intrigues[.]

It is time now to look into the particular Conduct of our own Colonies towards the Indians; and seeing a friendly convenient and beneficial Commerce is the surest basis of Alliances with them, whereon most of those Colonies have rested their Dependance for their Security, to consider what methods they have pursued for well regulating the Same, so [as] to answer that end. As [I] propose to confine my remarks chiefly to the Conduct and Management of the [7] Province of South Carolina (including Georgia), having to do with by far the most numerous Nations (above three times as many Indians as all the rest of the Colonies have to do with) with which I am best acquainted, and which being at least as good as the management of any other, will be sufficient to give a pretty just Idea of the whole, I shall say but little of that of the rest. *North Carolina*, having not hitherto carried on any Commerce with the Cherokees behind it, consequently hath left the regulation thereof intirely to South Carolina posessed of their whole Trade; and therefore hath no Law relating to the same. *Virginia* till within those few years past had little or no Concern with the Indian Trade, and was not visited by Indians nor at any standing Expence about them. That province, *Maryland*, and *Pensilvania*, which traffick of late Years with the Colonies of the six Nations and their dependants living on their backs, upon the Waters of the Ohio, have no Law for Regulation of the Trade, except a Law made by Pensilvania to prohibit the Carrying Rum to their Towns (upon a Complaint from the Indians themselves of the great Quantity brought among [them], desiring it might be stopt) and also the trafficking with Indians but *at their dwelling Houses, except by Persons recommended to, and Licenced by the Governor*. Every man that pleases goes from those Provinces among those Indians, and makes what he can of them in his own

The Methods taken by our several Colonies for regulating the Commerce with the Indians, whereon they have depended for their security.

vizt.
No. Carolina

Virginia.

Maryland &
Pensylvania.

---

15 Adair shares Atkin's fear of the influence of the priests over the Indians. *Adair's History*, p. 86.

THE
REPORT

New York

way; being under no Inspection or Controul. Sometimes the Traders of one Province set them against those of another. So that the greatest Disorders have arisen. Upon special Occasions Commissioners are sent from Virginia, and Maryland, to meet the Chiefs of the Six Nations at Lancaster in Pensylvania,[16] or from all three Provinces to Albany in New York, to treat with them, make up Differences, and the like. The Province of *New York* in which the Six Nations living by Cataracui or Ontario Lake depend, and which is capable of Furnishing them with Goods at near half the price that the French can from Mon[t]real (but whether it is done is a Question) permits any one that 'enters into a Bond to pay certain Duties on Goods, and Rum, or other strong Liquors for the use of those Indians, and not to defraud, or injure them, to trade with them either in their own Country, or at the Town of Albany; and hath committed the regulation of the Trade, and the chief management of Indian Affairs, to certain Commissioners living at Albany (the long accustomed place of Indian Interviews, and Treaties with that Government); who being the principal Persons concerned in that Trade by Permission, it cannot be wonder'd at if their measures are directed more by their own than the British Interest; and the Gross and horrible Impositions or Abuses, allowed on all hands to have been for a long course of Years committed by the Traders upon the Indians, unredressed. Mr Colden of his Majesty's Council of New York,[17] in the course of his History of those Nations, laments our not having any persons of Experience ever among them; and frequently mentions the prejudice done to our Interest among them, by the Neglect and Misconduct of those Commissioners. To which cause he in a great measure attributed in particular, the dissatisfied and wavering State of those Nations, and their suspicious Behaviour in Favour of the French in the Year 1746, when the Governor was directed to engage them to joyn in the Expedition intended against Canada. At which time the Oneydoes [18] having at first

---

[16] There is evidence to confirm Atkin's criticisms of the Pennsylvania traders in *Pennsylvania Archives* (1st series) Vols. I and II. For the Lancaster treaties see Carl Van Doren and Julian P. Boyd (eds.), *Indian Treaties Printed by Benjamin Franklin, 1736-1762* . . . (Philadelphia, 1938).

[17] Cadwallader Colden (1688-1776), philosopher, scientist, and lieutenant governor of New York published his *The History of the Five Indian Nations* . . . in 1727. It was later reprinted and enlarged.

[18] Or Oneida. Other tribes of the Six Nations were the Mohawk, the Onondaga, the Cayuga, the Seneca, and the Tuscarora.

refusd, even to give an Answer to his Invitation to meet him at
Albany, and the Cayugas having also refused to meet him there,
those Commissioners being applied to by the Governor declared,
*"They knew not any Person of Influence or Interest with the
Indians fit to send* [among] *them* on that occasion, being in a
bad Disposition, and much under the influence of the French".
The people were dissatisfied with the conduct of the Commissioners.[19] They themselves were divided [8] in Sentiments,
several refus'd to attend their meetings; and they confess'd to
the Governor, *they had lost all Influence on the Indians.* Their
policy seems to have been limited to their own private Convenience, to the drawing all Indians whatever with their Trade
to Albany, and occasionally to the trading Houses at Fort Oswego,[20] at a small Distance from thence, situated close by the
Lake Ontario in the country of the Six Nations. As they left
the Indian Trade almost intirely in the hands of the French at
Montreal, whom they furnished from Albany with our Goods to
carry it on, until the Year 1720, when the inhabitants of New
York were prohibited by Law to sell Indian Goods for the future
to the French; and those Trading Houses were established on
that Lake; by which means our Trade and Interest with the
Indians were exceedingly augmented; So since that time, they
[have] left the French in possession of the Trade upon all the
other four great Western Lakes; trading only with those Indians
that come to Albany, or to those Trading Houses; and by whom
the whole Trade and Navigation on the Lakes is very impoliti-
cally sufferd to be carried on in Canoes. And having neglected
to build a Fort while they might have done it at Niagara Fall
[a little more remote between Lake Ontario & Lake Erie] (in
like manner as they have done at Crown Point), the [French]
by building a Fort[21] there have excluded the New Yorkers
themselves from going out of Lake Ontario, and have thereby
preserv'd the dependance of the many Indian Nations round
them; which otherways they could not have done. It hath been
much admir'd at, that the Six Nations being in strict Alliance
with us, and enjoying a more Beneficial Trade with us than
they could with the French, should yet permit them to build

---

[19] Because of the incompetence of the commissioners, William Johnson
was appointed on August 27, 1746, as commissary of stores and provisions
for the Indians fighting the French. *Johnson Papers*, I, 59-60.

[20] Constructed in 1727. *New York Colonial Documents*, V, 818, 820.

[21] Fort Niagara (Onyegra) was originally built by the French in 1687.
Ibid., III, 476; IX, 335.

that Fort, and that the Government of New York hath in vain done every thing since in their Power to induce them to remove it. But the Chief Secret is this. Those Indians receive great Benefit from that Fort; a great Number of them being constantly employed in carrying about three Leagues over the Carrying [Place], that immense Quantity of Packs of Furrs which come from all the upper lakes, and Countries to the Westward; for doing which they are well paid. The Consequence of the N. York Conduct is not only, that we have hitherto miss'd the Aquisition of a most extensive Commerce thro' the Lakes, and thereby Security to our Colonies; but the French have had an Opportunity, after first fixing a Fort on the South Side of Lake Erie to enter upon the River Ohio (the great Object of their fears, as a Channel for us into the Missisippi River); whereby the Safety of all our Neighbouring Colonies is greatly endanger'd. That the said Governmt, so contiguous to, and so long posess'd of the whole Trade of the Six Nations, could not or did not prevail on them to put a Stop thereto, is a sort of Demonstration that it is not posess'd enough of their Affections; which must be owing to bad Management. And it will be well if a Rivalship or Opposition that is arisen between the Merchants or Traders of the City of N. York and Albany, may not have some ill Effect at this Juncture. For Mr Colden in his History hath given Instances of our Interest among the Indians having Suffer'd heretofore by Party Quarrels in that Government. The Government of *New England*, on which the Eastern Indians depend, and who as I have been assur'd, including those in Nova Scotia do not exceed 300 Men, hath in order to prevent Impositions lodged the management of their Trade on the Publick Account in certain Persons chosen by the General Court to procure Goods, and others to dispose of them at established Truck Houses; who in exclusion of all private persons, supply the Indians with Goods at the rates set in the Invoices sent from Boston and take their Furrs at the Market price in Boston, which persons are chosen Annually; and render annually Accts. of their Proceedings; and are not to Trade for themselves. [9] They are to supply the Indians with [Rum in] such moderate Quantities as they shall think Convenient. This hath the appearance of a very good Regulation. But yet without having Recourse to the same Principle of some Misconduct or other, it is scarce possible to account for the well known Indifference, and Disaffection of those Indians. A small Quantity of Goods

New England

in one or two Truck houses, one would think should be sufficient for those few Indians, But the truth is that being employed as Traders for Peltry between N. England and Canada, a vast deal of our Goods is introduced thro' their hands to Montreal; by which means, together with the Clandestine Trade carried on thither thro' the same kind of Channel from Albany, the French are now again upon as good a Footing, nay by means also of Niagara Fort which commands the passage to the four upper Lakes, superiour to what they were before the Act passed at N. York in 1720 [22] "for the encouragement of the Indian Trade, and rendering it more Effectual to the Inhabitants of that Province; and for prohibiting the selling of Indian Goods to the French" on the preamble to which Act it was declared, "That it was found by Experience, that the French of Canada, by means of Indian Goods brought from that Province, had not only almost wholly engrossed the Indian Trade, but had in a great measure withdrawn the Affections of the five Indian Nations from the Inhabitants of that Province, and renderd them wavering in their Allegiance to his Majesty; and would, if such Trade were not prevented, altogether alienate the minds of the said Indians, which would prove of dangerous Consequence to the English Interest in America." Within four Years after (in 1724) a Committee of the Council in New York said in a Report upon the purport of a Petition presented by some Merchants in London to the King against the renewal of that Act, "That whatever might be said of the Severity and Penalties therein, they were found insufficient to deter some from carrying Goods clandestinely to the French. And that the Legislature of that Province was convinc'd no Penalties could be too Severe to prevent a Trade, which put the Safety of all his Majesty's Subjects of North America in the greatest Danger." The Goods carried to Canada from New England, must certainly produce the same Consequences, as those carried from N. York. And therefore 'tis in vain to put a stop to that Trade from one Province, unless it be done in the other also.

I come back now to the Province of South Carolina. The place of Interviews and Treaties with Indian Chiefs is at Charles Town, from whence a Trade is carried on among several Numerous and Independent Nations, by Horse Carriage only, Eight Hundred Miles. To wit, the Catawbas, Cherokees, Creeks, Chicasaws; and not long since the Chactaws also. That Government

So Carolina

---

22 The ineffectiveness of this act is confirmed in *ibid.*, V, 745.

hath appointed a Commissioner for regulating the Trade with the Indians in Friendship therewith, conformable to the particular directions of An Act made for Preserving Peace, and continuing a good Correspondence and for regulating the Trade with them. Which hath been revived, and alter'd from time to time; the last Act in force being passed in April 1739 and the present Act in May 1752.[23] Since the fatal experience of the Indian War in 1715 which was occasioned by the Dealings of an Agent,[24] the said Commissioner, and every Agent at any time to be sent among the Indians, hath been and is strictly prohibited to sell any Indian Trading Goods to any Indian or [10] other Trading Person whatsoever; or to receive any Presents from any Indians, or Traders without the Leave of the Legislature, other than Provisions for his Subsistence while among them. No Person is allowed to Trade with any of them without a Licence from the Commissioner; who is required to give one to every Person applying, of honest Repute, and Sober Conversation; having publish'd their Names ten days at his office, and no just Cause appearing to the Contrary, and giving Bond for £200 Proclama. Money[25] with Suerity that he, and the Men (of like Character) employed to go with him, whose Names are to be inserted in his Licence, will demean themselves well towards the Indians; and that he will Obey and Observe all Orders and Instructions given him from time to time by the Commissioner; who is to give him at first going Instructions annex'd to his Licence, agreeable to the Law, under his hand and Seal of Office. And he is to insert in the Licence the Nation, and if it be among the Cherokees, or Creeks, the particular Town or Towns wherein such Trader intends and is permitted to Trade; but is not to transgress those Limits; allotting to each Trader two or more Towns, if one be too small; so that the whole be equally di-

[23] These acts are in Cooper, *Statutes at Large of South Carolina*, III, 517-25, 763-71.

[24] Atkin's statement, like other contemporary analyses of causes of the war, is misleading (Crane, *Southern Frontier*, p. 165). According to Crane, this was ". . . a far-reaching revolt against the Carolina trading régime. . . ." The natives also resented the general intrusion of cattle raisers. Indian agent John White, whom Atkin mentions, ". . . maintained great state among the Indians, requiring them 'to wait on [him] and carry his Lugage and packs of skins from one town to another purely out of Ostentation. . . .'" *Southern Frontier*, pp. 162-67.

[25] £100 sterling was equivalent to £133½ proclamation money. W. Roy Smith, *South Carolina as a Royal Province, 1719-1776* (New York, 1903), p. 279. The value of South Carolina's paper money was "one-seventh that of sterling." Meriwether, *Expansion of South Carolina*, p. 9.

vided among the several Traders. Those Licences are to be in force only one Year (except in the Chicasaw or Chactaw Nation, 18 Months) and to expire in March, April, May, or June; in one of which months every Trader is to come annually to Charles Town and take out a new Licence in Person as before; During which absence he may leave any one of the Men employed by him and named in his Licence, to take Care of his Storehouse & Goods; and empower him the mean while to Trade with the Goods so left in his Custody. But neither of them is at any other time to traffick with any Indian by any ways whatsoever. The Commissioner, or any Agent at any time sent by the Government, is empower'd and required to hear & determine all Complaints between any Indians and Traders; And to award to any Indian damages not exceeding £5 Proclama Money; And to agree with and employ Interpreters, and to swear them to Interpret faithfully the Talks and Discourses between the said Commissioner or Agent and any Indians; to the end that the Indian Trade may be the better Order'd and Settled, and that the Complaints of the Indians may be fully heard or understood, and their Grievances if any happen may be effectually redressed; And also to hire Messengers and Horses upon Emergencies, to send Express to the Commander in Chief, or to give Notice to the Inhabitants in case of Danger; the charge of which Interpreters and Messengers is to be paid out of the publick Treasury. And the said Commissioner is to do in all cases relating to the Indian Trade, as the Law directs, and is most conducive to the Good of that Province; And is also to observe such directions as from time to time he shall receive from the Governor and Council, or the General Assembly, and not otherways [except] in cases of an extraordinary [nature] wherein the immediate safety of that Province is Concern'd, and not directed and provided in that Act. So far the Act in force before May 1752, and the Act then passed and in force since, are alike.[26] I shall have occasion presently to observe some things wherein they differ.

From this Sketch, as by Implication it must be understood, that it is a part of the Business of the said Commissioner of Indian Affairs in So. Carolina, to visit some if not all the Nations from time to time, to Inquire into the Conduct of the Traders, to hear any complaints of the Indians, and to redress

Observations at large on the Regulation, & the Practices in the said Province

---

[26] Confirmed in the statutes. See note 23.

Grievances, it ought to be concluded that the managemt of the Indian Trade and Traders among the Southern Nations is well regulated and secured. But the case in Fact is just the Reverse. The Commissioner not being obliged by express Words in the Act to visit those Nations, nor any allowance having been established for that Service, altho it hath been one of his standing Instructions given to the Traders with their Licences, "That they are to take Notice, that he intended to visit the several Garrisons as often as occasion should require, in order to hear and redress any Complaints that should be made to him", [11] yet no Commissioner hath gone to either Nation, or to any Place convenient for the Purpose, ever since the Year 1735; when the then Commissioner was sent by the Government to the Creek Nation in Quality of an Agent, upon a particular Occasion. And since that time, Agents have been sent only twice to the same Nation, and twice to the Cherokee Nation, on sudden and extraordinary Occasion.[27] Tis True, by a Clause in the Act passed in 1752, setting forth "that since the Commissioner had not been obliged by law to go into the Indian Nations, many Irregularities had been committed by the Traders and other Persons, from whence great Terror and Disturbance had been brought upon his Majesty's Subjects, and the expenses for Indians greatly augmented"; He is therefore required under pain of forfeiting his office to go to any of the Nations (the Chicasaws and Chactaws by reason of their Distance excepted) But then it is at the same time limited thus, "whenever he should be ordered so to do by the Governor with the advice of the Council". And an allowance for that Service is indeed also specified payae. out of the Publick Treasury to him (fifty six Shilling Proclamation Money pr Diem for himself and two servants) or if he shall refuse or be unable to perform it to any other Person appointed by the Governor with advice of the Generall Assembly if sitting; and if not, with advice of the Council. But then there is no provision of a Fund for the payment of that money, or of any other Expence attending his

---

[27] Only one agent's journal is recorded in "Indian Books of South Carolina," Vols. II-IV (1750-1754). This is Abraham Bosomworth, Creek agent. See *ibid.*, III, 23 ff., IV, 40 ff. James Maxwell, Cherokee agent, and James Bullock, Creek agent, have a record of their journals in 1741 in *S.C. Assembly Journals, 1741-1742,* pp. 53, 330, 337. Colonel George Pawley's journal is noted in "Journal of the Commons House of Assembly," Vol. XXII (1746-1747).

Journey; which therefore still depends upon the Assembly; whose Spirit the Council is too well accquainted with, to advise the Governor to send the Comissioner, without first consulting them, when it can possibly be done. The Assembly if they differ in opinion or Disposition with the Council, in order to excuse themselves from providing the payment on any particular Occasion, will it may be presumed according to Custom if they have an Opportunity to do it in time, declare themselves against the Necessity of sending him; or afterwards, soon after his Arrival in any Nation, and the least favourable account of his Reception & Negotiation or Posture of Affairs, address the Governor to recall him immediately, merely to put a stop as soon as possible to the Expence. On so precarious a footing, no fit person can see it worth their while to turn their Backs suddenly upon their private Affairs to engage in such Service.

Without saying how far the Commissioners themselves have strictly observed the directions of the Law, with respect to the Traders, out of about twenty useful and Necessary Instructions given with their Licences, respecting their Behaviour towards the Indians, the Government, and to each other, which are fram'd agreeable to the express directions of that Law, and to long Experience, and which they give Bond to observe, I verily believe that not one hath been, or is duly observd by them all. And no Inspection or Inquiry being made into their Behaviour by the Commissioner on the Spot in any one of the Nations, information can come only from among the Traders themselves; who being all more or less Culpable, altho the one half of the several Penalties inflicted by the Law are given to him that shall Sue for the same, it cannot be imagined that any of them will in many Cases either give information or Offences, or support the Commissioner in the proof thereof. Accordingly I have never known any Penalty for a particular Offence sued for, nor any Bond Sued to a Recovery of the Penalty. So that the Law for regulating the Indian Trade is almost a dead Letter; and the Commissioner of little more use than going thro' the mere form of giving Licences to Traders, and taking Bonds for the Observance of Instructions, which not being duly enforced are so little Regarded, that the present Commissioner declared once to a Committee, That in the Space of a full Year then pass'd, he had received from all the Traders in all the Nations, conformable to those Instructions, only three Letters of Intelligence and no Journal at all of their Proceedings.[28]

[12] The Evils arising from the Commissioner's not making a personal Enquiry into the Behaviour of the Traders in some Convenient place or other, are very great. Besides their Neglect or Breach of their particular Instructions, in every which Case the public is consequently more or less affected, they cheat the Indians most abominably both in Weight and Measure; as well as otherways abuse them (against which things indeed tis remarkable their is no Instruction, nor—Penalty by Law) And no check being put upon their avarice, they exact what [Rates] they please for Goods. The principal Offences of the Traders against the Act of 1739 by breach of their Instructions, whereby the publick was most Affected, were, Vizt— 1st. Their not [only] Transgressing themselves the Limits prescribed by their Licences, but permitting and employing their Servants, even Pack horse Men, whom they have sent to and left in Towns alone, to trade with the Indians; whose Behaviour, being for the most part the most worthless of Men, is more easy to be conceived than described. In particular some of the Chief Persons concerned in the Creek Trade, united in a Company, and the Principal if not sole Creditors of the rest engaged in that and the Chicasaw Trade, had, and I suppose still have Licences in their own Names for Towns where they seldom resided, but kept Servants to do their Business. Whereas they were allowed by the said Act, "only to leave and empower one of their Men to dispose of any Goods left in his Custody, while they should go to Charles Town to renew their Licences"— 2d. Their bringing the Indians into Debt, by giving them large Credit for Goods, whereas they were prohibited "to Trust or Credit any one Indian beyond the Value of Six Deer Skins, or nine Pounds weight of Leather; that is for one Pound of Powder and four Pounds of Bulletts;"[29] being sufficient to fit him out

---

[28] There appears to be no record in the journals of the council of Indian Commissioner William Pinckney's making this statement. Pinckney was reappointed commissioner in 1752 ("Council Journals," Vol. XVIII [1751-1752], p. 302) and has a memorial concerning the inefficiency of the trading act of 1739 recorded in *ibid.*, Vol. XVII (1748-1750), p. 388. No journals of the traders appear in the "Indian Books," but there is one letter concerning Cherokee affairs in "Council Journals," Vol. XVIII (1751-1752), pp. 428 ff. The traders' correspondence seems to come under the headings of petitions or complaints, rather than "Intelligence."

[29] The act of 1739 limits Indian credit to only "six buck-skins." No mention is made of leather, powder or bullets. See Cooper, *Statutes at Large of South Carolina*, III, 521.

for War or Hunting. The pernicious Consequences of which larger Credit, are no less than these. It gives the Traders an undue Influence over such Indians in matters of Public Concern; It discourages the Indians from Hunting for Deer Skins and other Furrs, and renders them indolent, seeing in such Case the Product of their Labour is to go to pay only for what is past; If they are tempted with the same, instead of paying their Debts; to purchase supplies for their present or Future Wants, it thence produces Quarrels between them and the Traders; by which the Provincial Peace and Safety is Hazarded, seeing according to the Nature of Indian Governmt. the Nation is often involved in the Consequences of the Act of any Single Man. It also inclines the Young Fellows to mischief, and is an inducement with them in certain Conjunctures to break out War with us, or to Desert us, as being the surest and easiest method of Cancelling their Debts, when too heavy for them. That Principle was one of the Causes of some of the five Nations first removing to near Montreal. It was also, after the Chactaws had revolted from the French to us in the late War,[30] one of the Causes of the first ten of their Towns revolting back again at one time. And it had liked to have produc'd the same kind of Effect latterly among the Cherokees and Creeks at different Times— 3d. Their Trading with the Albama French Garrison in the upper Creek Nation even in the time of the late War between us and the French; and also with the Chactaws after they had revolted back to the French. Whereas they were strictly prohibited, "not to presume to Trade or traffick with any Indian or Indians in Enmity with his Majesty's Subjects, nor with the Subjects of any Foriegn Prince, under pain of Forfeiting their Bonds and being rendered forever incapable of having a Licence to Trade with the Indians". The most pernicious Consequence attended the free, and I may say Friendly Trade, carried on with the Albama Garrison by some of Creek Traders, during the late War. [13] At that time the French in Louisiana, being by the Course of the War without Supplies from France, were not only unable to supply any of the Indians with Goods, but even their own Garrisons with Cloathing and other Necessaries; the state and Condition of which at last was such, that they had not Ammunition left sufficient for making a Defence in case of an Attack. The Chactaws at that juncture threw themselves Naked into our Arms, and implored our Re-

---

[30] See the account of Atkin's Choctaw revolt essay in the Introduction.

lief, Protection & Friendship; And as a proof of their Fidelity made a Voluntary Offer not only to take Tambekbe Fort in their Nation by Surprize,[31] but to assist the Creeks in taking the Albama Fort. At that very time those Creek Traders not only supplied the wants of the Men of that Garrison, and also goods for Mobile, but furnished some of the very Presents which the French gave the Creek Indians in support of their Interest. And while the So. Carolina Government Meditated an Expedition against that Fort, those Traders so far discouraged it one way or other, that when the Chactaws were returning homeward who had been down to Charles Town and made a new Treaty of Peace and Commerce, partly on Condition of the aforesaid Offer, the Commanding Officer at Fort Moore[32] on Savana River wrote to the Governor, "That it was reported they had chang'd their minds as to the taking that Fort; which must have been put into their Heads; because upon enquiry he found that the Demolishing of it would be a disadvantage to some who were engaged in the Trade". The friendly Commercial Intercourse between our Traders and the Albama Garrison, was thought by the French of so much Importance to their Interest at that Conjuncture, that they never at any time during a Peace between the two Crowns discovered so amicable a Disposition towards our Traders, as they did then while we were at War; when they countenanced and promoted a principle among the Indians, That it was good for them to be at Peace, and Trade with both the English and the French— With respect to our Traders trading with the Chactaws after the Commencement of their Rupture with us, the ill Consequence was the loss to the King, of the Lives and Property of some of his Majesty's Subjects, which might otherwise have been saved. Besides the tendency to make those Indians regardless of publick Treaties, seeing they could still have the Goods they wanted, and for which they courted our Friendship, from Private Traders independant of the Government.

If the Publick Service was affected by the Offences of the Traders against the Act of 1739, under the three foregoing Heads, it cannot but be still more greatly affected by the alterations made in those points in the present Act passed in 1752.

---

[31] Fort Tombigbee or Tombecbe was erected by the French in 1736 on the river of the same name. Alden, *John Stuart*, p. 11.

[32] Fort Moore was constructed in 1716 on a bluff of the east bank of the Savannah River approximately six miles below the site of Augusta. Meriwether, *Expansion of South Carolina*, pp. 10-11.

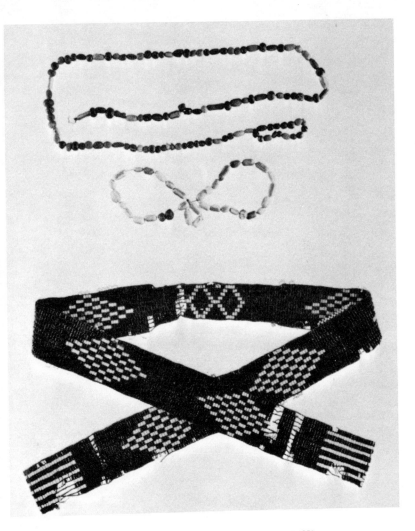

TRADE BEADS OF THE SOUTHERN INDIANS

AND

CREEK INDIAN WAMPUM BELT

(Courtesy Charleston Museum)

THE
REPORT

Remarkable
Alterations for
the worse, in the
late Act for
regulating the
Trade in So.
Carolina

25

Instead of being allowed as before only to leave and empower one of their Men to dispose of Goods left, while they should go to Charles Town to renew their Licences, the Traders are now permitted, "to reside only Six Months in the Towns for which they have Licences." By which means the worthless Fellows their Servants, are at Liberty to deal wholly with the Indians one half the Year. Instead of the Restraint upon the Credit to be given to any one Indian limited before to Six Deer Skins (or nine Pounds of Leather,) the Traders are now allowed, "to Credit any one Indian to the value of Twentyfour pounds of Leather to each Indian Man living in any Town or Towns inserted in his Licence" [33] [14] which Equivocal Expression may possibly be pretended, to extend the Credit of any one Indian further then 24 pounds of Leather; even to as many times that Value, as there are Men in his Town— And the prohibition before, not to Trade with any Indians in Enmity with his Majesty's Subjects, or with the Subjects of any Foreign Prince, is now intirely taken off, there being not one word said about it in the Act. Thus the French in Louisiana, have now a free open Trade with us for Indian trading Goods tolerated by Land and Sea; By Land with our Indian Traders, for the particular occasional Wants of their Garrisons; and by Sea at Mobile, as heretofore with the Merchants of Charles Town and N. York, for their Trade with the Indians; which Trade with Canada is carried on only Clandestinely. A Key might be found to those extraordinary alterations by the said Act, all in favour of the private Trader, to the prejudice of the Service of the Crown. But I wave it, as being foreign to the Design of these papers.

There is a Clause in the said Act worth Notice, touching a Subject never before mentioned in any former Act. "No person licenced to Trade with the Indians, *if he is a Cherokee Trader*, is to carry any Rum or other Spirituous Liquour to that Nation." [34] I forbear also to offer any Conjecture at the Reason of a Restraint so Conspicuously Partial; and shall leave it Wrapp'd up in its own Mysterious Air, with this Observation only, That were it founded wholly in a regard to the Welfare of the Indians and of that Province, inasmuch as Rum is alike hurtful and productive of the same Consequences in one Nation as in another, methinks the Restraint of carrying it shou'd have been extended to all the Traders to every Nation— This

---

[33] Confirmed in Cooper, *Statutes at Large of South Carolina*, III, 767.
[34] Confirmed in *ibid.*

gives occasion to say something of the general Effects of that Liquor, the too frequent use of which, with the permission or Neglect of our Colony Governments, hath destroyed more Indians than all their Wars put together have done; and whom yet, while they continue our Friends, it is our great Interest with the utmost care to Preserve. All Indians whatever are so passionately fond of Rum, as to be unable to withstand it. The most prudent of them resolving sometimes to give a loose to it, provide Centinels who are not to taste a drop the while, to prevent any mischief they may be inclined to do when Drunk. Their Reason or Will having no share therein, they have no Conception that they are culpable so far as to deserve to suffer for any mischief or outrage committed by them while in that Condition. If complained of, or upbraided for it, they say with great Composure, "that they are sorry for what hath happened, But that it was not they that did it, 'twas Rum did it". Yet being truly sensible of the great Evils produced from it by Quarrels and Acts of Violence, as well among themselves between the nearest Relations, as with the white People; they heartily lament in general the having ever known what Rum was; And have themselves pointed out to us the only Remedy possible, which is to withhold it from them. The Chiefs of every Nation finding the Evil daily encreasing, and their Young Men growing untractable in their National Concerns, have at times requested the Governours of our several Colonies to restrain the Indian Traders from carrying either too much Rum, or any at all among them. And accordingly N. England, N. York, and Pensylvania have passed Laws in different manners to restrain them from doing it. [In New York indeed Rum may however be carried to *Oswego* to trade, in any Quantities, paying a certain Duty.] But tis more than to be feared they have all by various ways been eluded; particularly that of Pensylvania, not only for want of some executive Power, to enforce it upon the Spot among the Indians, but because the Virginia & Maryland [*Merchants*] Traders who trade [15] with the same Indians, are not prohibited to carry Rum to them; these provinces having never passed any Law whatever, I apprehend, for the regulation of the Indian Trade, as they had not till very lately any Concern therein. But with respect to Carolina so long Concerned in it, and with so many Nations, whose Chiefs have often in my hearing at Public Audiences expressed their desire of a Restraint upon the carrying Rum among them, it cannot but appear surprising that that Province hath never taken any Step towards a Restraint upon carrying Rum among them, before this partial Restraint upon the Cherokee Traders; altho the ill Consequences of the Rum Trade [35] must in the Nature of things be much more Interesting among the Creeks, who are in the Neighbourhood of both French and Spaniards; whereas the Cherokees have seldom an opportunity of seeing any but Englishmen.

But to return to the Behaviour of the Traders. Being left to themselves in the several Nations without Controul, besides the offences they committ in the Trade against the positive directions of the Law, and their Instructions, they do other things whereby the Acts of Government are immediately affected; to wit, by sending false accounts of some things, and suppressing the knowledge of others, to serve their private purposes; by writing Letters in the name of Indians of Note; by talking with them too freely upon the Affairs of Government, and intermedling with their making Peace or War with one another; and by encouraging many to come to Charles Town without Leave, to pay visits on slender pretences, merely to get presents, which Actions often create very large Expences.

This neglected State of Affairs between the Indians & Traders, together with Some other Causes, hath within the last ten Years introduced not only the greatest Disorder in the several Indian Nations, but Perplexity in the measures of Government. The Province hath been kept under almost one continued State of Alarm and uneasiness. And consequently the Annual Indian Expences, have been augmented to a very great Degree beyond the former Amount of them.[36] Oftentimes within that space of

The bad
Consequences
of the Defects
in the Regulation
of the Indian
Commerce in
So Carolina.

---

[35] The famous Catawba chief, King Hagler, echoed Atkin's words in his indictment against the whites: "Brothers here is One thing You Yourselves are to Blame very much in, That is You Rot Your grain in Tubs out of which you take and make Strong Spirits You sell it to our young men and give it them, many times. . . ." Meriwether, *Expansion of South Carolina*, p. 142. The problem of the rum traders was not confined to the southern frontier. Sir William Johnson wrote that the Indians had become so accustomed to liquor its sale was "absolutely necessary . . . under certain restrictions." *New York Colonial Documents*, VII, 665. For a more extensive discussion of the rum trade, see Wilbur R. Jacobs, "Unsavory Sidelights on the Colonial Fur Trade," *New York History*, Vol. XXXIV (April, 1953), pp. 135-48.

[36] There is a steady increase in funds of "Indian Expenses" as recorded in the "Journals of the Commons House of Assembly." From March to December, 1758, "Indian Expenses" were £14,837 14s. 10½d., South Carolina currency. This figure does not include costs for fortifications or military defense. See "Journals of the Commons House of Assembly," Vol. XXXII (1757-1759), pp. 208-11. For records of 1749-1750, see note 43, below.

time the Assembly hath voted the necessity of sending Agents, in particular to the Cherokee and Creek Nation; yet an Agent hath been sent only once to each of them. On the most Interesting Occasions when the Governour resolved to send an Agent, I have never known that Government so distressed at any other time for anything else, as then to find a proper Person equal to the thing, or fit for the Purpose; and much more one who would undertake it. For almost all that had a Personal Knowledge of the Indians and their Affairs have been sometime gone off the Stage. And few indeed for other Reasons that might be given, have any tolerable Acquaintance with their real State and Transactions. Most of those to whom an Agency hath on such Occasions been offer'd at Different times, have refused to accept it;[37] upon different Motives, but chiefly because they thought the undertaking Hazardous, (as well as uncertain in Duration) and expected not to accomplish the Service proposed. The last and the present Commissioner for regulating the Trade, both declined it. The former even thought a Provision ought to be be made by the Publick for his Family in Case of his Death in the Service.

Inconveniences attending the Meetings of Indians in Charles Town.

Before I conclude these observations on the Regulation & Management of the Indian Trade in South Carolina, It is proper to say something of the Inconveniences attending the [*meetings*] Transaction of Publick Affairs between that Government & the Indians, [16] by Meetings in Charles Town. On those Occasions heretofore, according to the practice of the Eastern Nations of the World, there was an Exchange of Presents, (however small on the part of the Indians on Account of their Poverty yet) as expressive of the true footing upon which they met, a mutual Friendship. As the Visits have of latter Years become less National, and more Partial, and from Particular Towns only, the Practice hath for that and other Reasons been imprudently discontinued; and the Presents are now given on our Part only— As the Government in the situation before related, is under a Necessity of taking its information and Intelligence

---

[37] A careful search of the journals of the upper and lower houses and the "Indian Books" does not give evidence of the refusal of Indian "Agencies." The Indian agents were often members of the Assembly (e. g., James Bullock and James Maxwell), and it does not seem unreasonable that the legislators might refuse such appointments. There is record of one Captain H. Hyrne modestly accepting an agency to the Cherokee "unless prevented by Sickness, in which case I hope some other person may be found much more capable. . . ." "Indian Books of South Carolina," Vol. II, pp. 143, 153-54.

of the Indian Affairs almost intirely from the Indian Traders, whereby as I said before, its Acts or Measures are affected (being sometimes either kept in the Dark, or hurried into needless Expence just as it happens, there being nothing found so Difficult often times as to distinguish the Truth or Falsehood of their Intelligence); so when Indians come to Charles Town, Traders who write Letters by them, or come as Interpreters [38] with them, by their recommendations impose their own Favourites or Friends upon the Government as Leading Men, for the sake of Presents; by which means many Indians receive valuable Presents, who have really very little Influence in their Nation. Nay sometimes such receive by the same means Commissions also, which cannot but displease the Men of Superior Sway in their own Towns— Sometimes among a number of Indians that come, there is not more than one or two leading Men or Chiefs; yet all must have Presents. Sometimes they come to the Settlements without the leave heretofore Stipulated; and being come so far, it is not thought prudent to stop them. Nor is it practicable to limit their Number— And sometimes valuable Presents are given to a number of Indians that come, who all belong to one or two or at most three Towns of their Nations— In the mean while many of the old Creek Chiefs who bear great Sway among the Young Men, being unable to perform such a Journey, are forc'd to cringe to the French who live among them, for the sake of a few necessaries; Trifles— I had occasion before to observe, that when Indians of Consequence do receive valuable Presents from us, in their own Estimation they earn them dearly by fatiguing Journies of some hundred Miles, and the loss of time from their Hunts which would have turned to better Account for themselves, as well as for the Trade. Wherefore a small Present delivered in any Nation, would be far more acceptable than a very large one fetch'd from Charles Town. And at the same time as the same Value which is now given in Presents, would be thereby more diffus'd among our Friends, there would also be a saving to the Government of the Expence attending their coming down. There have not been wanting Traders to point this out to the Government; who have even suggested that every Trader should be obliged to carry up a Part of the Presents free of Charge; but proposing also, that the same should be distributed by such of them as might be most

---

[38] Lachlan McGillivray, the famous Creek trader, occasionally acted as an interpreter. "Journals of the Commons House of Assembly," Vol. XXIV (1749-1750), pp. 636-39, records £120, paper currency, for his services.

relied on. But this sort of Remedy would be worse than the Disease itself. For if any of the Traders were trusted with such a Distribution of Presents sent up to the Nations, besides that the Transaction itself would necessarily destroy [the natural & true] Ideas Indians have of Presents (that is, that they are given mutually as tokens of Friendship, when Friends meet upon Business of a National Concern), and consequently in time make them lookd on as a kind of Tribute from us; it can scarce be imagined but that such Traders would in that [17] Distribution have a great regard to their private Interest;[39] they would accquire all that Weight and Influence which is due only to a Government, (perhaps to it's prejudice); and the Government would gradually loose almost all Share in the real management & knowledge of Indian Affairs. If any other Person were sent by the Government on Purpose, meerly to make such a Distribution of Presents, and upon no other Business, the Case would be little Better; Because it must produce the same Effects in the Apprehensions of the Indians, and towards the Government in it's proper Weight, as well as it's Knowledge and Management of their Affairs— Another Inconvenience attending the Indian Meetings in Charles Town, is the Sickness contracted there by them from the great change of Air, but chiefly of the Water. The latter never fails after a Short stay to produce a remarkable Alteration in their Health; to which a freeer Diet also Contributes; which renders them very impatient to be gone again. Fevers and Fluxes [40] attack them soon after, and frequently carry off some in their return homeward. When long delayed in Town, which hath been too often the Case, many have shared that fate together. There are some other Inconveniences needless to enter into, arising from the imprudencies of some of their People as well as of our own, during their passing and repassing through our Settlements.

Of his Majesty's
Presents granted
in 1748

Having said so much of Presents, altho it may be a further Digression, yet as it may give some usefull Lights to your Lordships, I presume it will not be amiss to say something concerning the money heretofore granted by his Majesty for that use. In

---

[39] There is record of one Thomas Andrews, Chickasaw trader, who overcharged the South Carolina government £400, South Carolina currency, for "supplies" for the Chickasaw. *S.C. Assembly Journals, 1741-1742,* p. 420.

[40] Dysentery. The Indians also lived in fear of "Fevers," and were reluctant to visit colonial towns in the summer because of the "sickly season." Smallpox epidemics were the worst. The Chickasaw were severely stricken in 1749. "Council Journals," Vol. XVI (1747-1749), pp. 122-24.

1747 the Legislature of South Carolina representing to his Majesty, "that in order to keep up a good Understanding with several Nations of Indians, and to prevent the Influence of the French and Spaniards, that Province had been at a charge in Treaties and presents amounting generally to about Fifteen hundred Pounds Sterling Pr. Annum, prayed, that the future Expence of Presents for Indians, and of keeping them in his Majesty's Interest, might be defrayed by his Majesty in Ease of the then distress'd Inhabitants". The Year following his Majesty was pleased to direct, "That the Sum of three thousand Pounds Sterling should be annually sent from England, to be distributed in Presents to the Indians Contiguous to and in alliance with the Provinces of South Carolina and Georgia,[41] in such manner as the Governor, Council, and Assembly of South Carolina, in Conjunction with such Person as should be appointed by the Trustees for Georgia; should judge most for his Majesty's Service, and might best answer the intended purpose of securing the Friendship of those Indians. Such Distribution to be made by two Persons, to be appointed one by the said Governor Council and Assembly, and the other by the said Trustees; who were to act Jointly for that Purpose." [42] And in regard that those Presents might be had Cheaper in England than in America, it was thought Expedient to give Directions for buying and sending them over. That Sum, if not restrained wholly to Presents, had been capable of effecting very great Services. It furnished considerably more Presents than there was need of, without easing the People of So. Carolina of their Expences, according to the prayer of their Petition, and I presume his Majesty's gracious Intention; and without effecting the least additional Service more than before to the Crown. For by an Estimate of the whole particular Expences, in the four preceeding Years, the presents alone amounted to little more than £500 Sterling pr. annum, one Year with the other.[43] The rest of the Expences

---

[41] Confirmed in *ibid.*, pp. 51-57, Report on the Duke of Bedford's letters, May 27, 1749; "Report of the Committee Concerning Presents Granted to the Indians of South Carolina and Georgia," May 30, 1749, LO 174.

[42] "Council Journals," Vol. XVI (1747-1749), pp. 51-57, confirm this. See also manuscript index of Vol. XVI for legislative discussion of these presents.

[43] The "Journals of the Commons House of Assembly" have an annual "Estimate of Public Debt" which represented creditors' claims against the government. Vol. XXV (1749-1750), pp. 636-39, contains the first classified expenditures, and here the expenses "For Indians" total £7429 1s. 9d., South Carolina currency—about £1061 sterling. This money does not

arose from the entertainment of Indians in their Visits, the payment occasionally of Rangers, Expresses, Interpreters, an Agent &c; which therefore still remained to be Discharged by Taxes. And if it was intended that the different Indians should be sent for on Purpose to receive the whole Presents, (which tho' thought improper was doubted), those Taxes must have been [18] encreased thereby. And with respect to Georgia, altho' in the time of the War, Indians were encouraged by the commanding Officer of the Kings Regiment of Foot Soldiers, to attend the same often at Frederica;[44] Yet after the Conclusion of the Peace in Europe, and the disbanding that Regiment, there being no Skin Trade carried on from Savanna, only a few stragling Indians, chiefly Creeks and Chicasaws of that River, resorted thither. On arrival of the said presents in 1749 at Charles Town (being consigned by the Purchasers to the Governor, Council, and Assembly for the use of the two Persons who were to distribute them), Instructions appeared from the Trustees of Georgia to the President, (the person appointed by them to act in Conjunction[)], "That a store was to be kept at Charles Town and another at Savanna for the Reception of one Moiety of each Species of Presents to each Store; that for Savanna under his Care, and that at Charles Town under the care of the Person to be appointed to act with him on behalf of So. Carolina. And that each of them was to give the other notice to attend the Distribution of any Presents given to the Indians". And it appearing further [that] conformable to the direction of the Trustees, notice had been sent from Georgia to the Creeks some Months before of the Presents intended for them, the Governor, Council and Assembly in compliance with their Sense, and to prevent any Censure or ill Consequence that might attend the coming down of the Indians to Savannah in expectation of Presents, consented to deliver a moiety of every species of the said Presents to the Person sent for them; which were carried to Savannah accordingly. By means of that Division and separate Distribution, the same Indians had part of those Presents in both Places, without its answering more than the same End. As the people of Georgia had little or no personal Communication with any other Indians than the Creeks, the most of their moiety fell to that Nation,

---

represent presents alone, but also expenditures for interpreters, entertainment of Indians, and other charges connected with Indian affairs. Fortifications were still another expense, amounting to £1446 12s. 6d., South Carolina currency. Expenses for Indians doubled by 1758. See note 36.

[44] The fort at Frederica, Georgia.

which yet partook of the other moiety of So. Carolina, which had by means of its trade to do with more Nations. And a good opportunity was lost, for uniting by a joint Distribution of the Presents the Interest of the two Provinces, and for destroying the ridiculous Distinction and Impressions raised by the contending Traders; which method could not but have tended also, to lessen the Expence of both in time to come— a Person[45] recommended by the Secretary of State to be appointed Agent on the part of the Governor, Council and Assembly of So. Carolina, for the Distribution of the Presents, was sent to Savannah to act in Conjunction with the Agent of the Trustees,[46] in the Distribution of the Moiety there. The Moiety at Charles Town was distributed (under Direction of the Governor, Council, and Assembly) by the Commissary of the Province; who was the proper Officer for providing and Delivering Presents to the Indians and for entertaining them. It was impossible that both Agents could joyn at the same time in both Provinces. If the two Persons directed to be appointed had been named *Storekeepers*, for receiving, and keeping Account of the delivery of the Presents, pursuant to Orders, it would have been Clear. But the words, *Agent* and *Distribution*, occasioned that it was not well Comprehended; as they seemed to imply some discretionary Power in themselves, not very proper in their Situation, or compatible with that of the respective Governments. For the Impropriety, Inconvenience, and Impracticability in general of the method prescribed, with regard to the said Presents, I beg leave to refer to a Report which was made in So. Carolina from a Committee of Conference appointed to take into Consideration the Letters of his Grace the Duke of Bedford, his Majesty's then principal Secretary of State, and other Papers relating to the Distribution of the said Presents; which may be seen in the Journals of the Council and Assembly.[47]

It remains now in order to perfect the View of the Regulation and [19] Management of the Indian Trade in our several Colonies, to speak of that in Georgia; which being but a part of So. Carolina separated, and put under a distinct Government, is situated alike to the same Indians, but rather

Regulation of the Trade in *Georgia.*

---

[45] Abraham Bosomworth. See "Council Journals," Vol. XVI (1747-1749), p. 39; Candler, *Colonial Records of the State of Georgia*, XXVI, 174.

[46] Patrick Graham, acting for William Stephens. "Council Journals," Vol. XVI (1747-1749), p. 55.

[47] See note 41 for references to the above committee.

nearer; the Traders who go to any of them from Charles Town, except the Catawbas and Cherokees, being obliged to pass thro' it. Licences to Trade were given annually at Savannah as at Charles Town, under the authority of the Trustees while their charter lasted, by the President as Commissioner for that purpose. The Instructions given therewith I never saw. Whatever they were, the Observance of them was not better enforced by any measures taken for the purpose, than that of those given in Charles Town. The proper Inhabitants or Settlers of that infant Colony, from their Inability in point of Substance and much nearer Concern to attend their own present Subsistence and future Provision, have hitherto had little or no Commerce with the Indians in European Goods. Their natural Connection and Intercourse is with the lower Creeks. Almost all who obtain'd Licences at Savannah to Trade with them, or their next Neighbours the Cherokees, were such of the Traders of So. Carolina as applied for them, being unwilling to return, either at first in order to avoid Payment of certain Duties once laid upon Skins, or of Penalties incurr'd; or afterwards to shun their Creditors; or because they were refused Licences, or at least could not obtain them for such Towns as they wanted them. Most of those also who Traded from Augusta (on the Path to the Creeks and other Nations, a little above Fort Moore on Savannah River the usual Embarkadear of the Trade) were Traders of So. Carolina, who to save the trouble and Inconvenience of Passing and Repassing that River every time with their Goods and Horses, built Storehouses and other Houses there; Yet still took their Licences from Charles Town, from whence they had their trading Goods, and to which place they sent the Skins in return by Water. The Traders licenced by the two Provinces for the same Nations, interfered with one another even in the same Towns; and set the Indians against each other (in like manner as the Pensylvania and Virginia Traders did [not] long since). A Dispute arose in regard to the Boundaries of Georgia according to the Charter, whether the lower Cherokee Towns were within it or not, and Consequently what Laws ought to operate or be put in force there.[48] Seizures were attempted to be made there. The Indians interposed, asking if they did not all belong to one King? The two Provinces let drop their Authority, neither calling their own, or the other Traders to account for their Offences. Nor was any amicable

---

[48] Governor Glen claimed that part of South Carolina was "southward of Georgia." "Council Journals," Vol. XVI (1747-1749), p. 85.

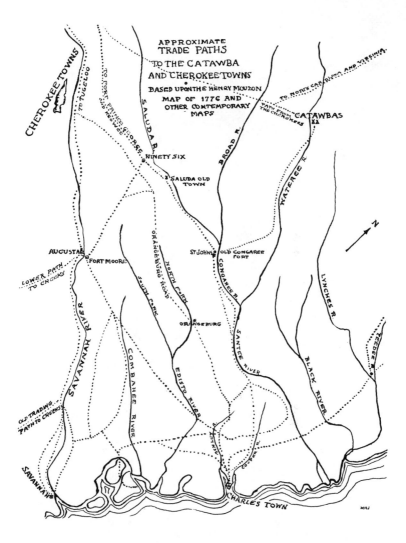

APPROXIMATE TRADE PATHS TO THE CATAWBA AND CHEROKEE TOWNS

(Based upon the Henry Mouzon Map of 1776 and Other Contemporary Maps)

Expedient ever fallen on to exert joyntly their Power for that Purpose, or to prevent the respective Traders interfereing, by sharing the Towns or otherways. Between the Licenced Traders of both Provinces, to the scandal of both Governments in the Eyes of the Indians, a third sort started up without any Licences at all; more especially among the Cherokees, not only from So. Carolina and Georgia, but from Virginia, near the Bounds of which some part of the Cherokee Country [certainly] is, which extends at least from the Latitude of 34 to 36.[49] And if Traders were to go there also from No. Carolina, within the supposed Bounds of which a great part of that Country undoubtedly is, the present Disorders would be encreased if possible by so many Different Traders accountable to different Powers, under different Regulations, or none at all. The unlicenced Traders, being the lowest People, having little thought of paying their Creditors for their Goods, often greatly undersell the fair Licenced Traders, which makes the Indians very uneasy, suspecting therefrom that the latter wrong them— But the greatest Disorders, and the most pernicious Consequences of all, have been introduced by the many Traders licenced and unlicenced, who have made a constant Practice of [carrying] very little Goods, but chiefly, and for the most part intirely *Rum* from Augusta;[50] from whence as soon as the Indian Hunters are expected in from their Hunts, they set out [20] with small or large Quantities of that bewitching Liquor according to their Ability, for the Creeks and Cherokees, but chiefly the latter Nation, to which they get in four Days. Then some of those Rum Traders place themselves near the Towns, in the way of the Hunters returning home with their deer Skins. The poor Indians in a manner fascinated, are unable to resist the Bait; and when Drunk are easily cheated. After parting with the fruit of three or four Months Toil, they find themselves at home, without the means of buying the necessary Clothing for themselves or their Families. Their Domestick and inward Quiet being broke, Reflection sours them, and disposes them for Mischief. To the same cause is owing, that the Quality of their Leather is Debased. For those Rum Traders take any Skins, badly dressed, and untrimmed; which require one Horse the more in 5 or 6 to carry them, and harbour Worms that daily destroy them. And the Indians

---

49 The "Map of the Southern Indian District. . . ." by Joseph Purcell [1773], W. L. Clements Library, confirms Atkin's location of the Cherokee country.

50 Confirmed by *Adair's History*, p. 394 n.

require the other Traders in their Towns to take them in the same Condition— The case is no better with the Rum Trade in the Towns. The great plenty of it hath produced Disorders unknown; and a licentiousness hath crept in among [the young] men, beyond the Power of the Head Men to Remedy. The Traders are insulted by them, their Horses stolen, their Goods pilfer'd, and Rum taken away, sometimes openly by force. The discreet Old men Censure alike their own Young Men and us. To Compleat the Scene of Confusion in the Lower Cherokee Nation, a Parcel of Vagabond Horse Pedlars from the back parts of the Northern Countries, rendezvous and harbour there; of whom the Nation wants much to be purged. In a word the wisest Indians among the Creeks and Cherokees, who have taken much Notice of those things, have expressed their Apprehensions that it must end in a Rupture between them and us.

Remarks on the
Management of
the Colonies
in General.

My Lords I have now gone through the Regulation and Management of the Indian Trade and Commerce, in our Several Colonies that have any Concern therein; which Trade is so closely connected and interwoven with the Affairs of Government, that it cannot be separted from them. And I flatter myself that what I first suggested is now very Apparent, That the British Interest among the Indian Nations in alliance with us, as it hath done for some Years past, must on the present footing, in the very nature of things, continue to decline while we have any to lose. And Consequently that there is an absolute Necessity for putting all the Indian Affairs immediately under some new and general Direction.

the Consequences
&
Necessity of a
new & general
Direction of the
Indian Affairs.

While the French have with great Care and Pains, by every method, cultivated the Friendship of the Indians in General, in the midst of them, & secured a footing by Forts, wherever they could have the least opening to do it, the Nations in Alliance with our Colonies, have been too much neglected, and left exposed not only to their and our Enemies, but a Prey to the Avarice of [a] contemptible set of Traders. There hath not only no Fort been yet built in any of the Indian Nations in all that great Extent of Territory to the Southward of the proper country of the Six Nations,[51] (and Fort Oswego is very insufficient to protect them on the Borders of Lake Ontario, by which the French are constantly Passing and repassing); But not even any

---

[51] Later, following Braddock's defeat, especially during the year 1756, a whole string of forts appeared along the southern frontier. See Koontz, *The Virginia Frontier*, pp. 111-48.

effectual method hath yet been taken to secure their good usage in their Dealings [with us]. Insomuch that the French have gone so far as to upbraid our Indians with a plain appeal to Facts, "That we neither build Forts for their Protection, nor [21] mend their Guns and Hatchets for them, as they do; That we set no Account by any of them, but Hunters for the sake of Skins; And that our Traders Cheat & impose upon them." And they have plainly shewn by their late proceedings on the back of Virginia and Pensylvania, that they think matters already ripe for them to reap the full Benefit of the Mismanagement and neglect of our Colonies. The Conduct of the Six Nations on this Occasion, hath too well justified them in that way of thinking. I have but one remark more to make in support of a new regulation of the Indian Affairs; founded upon the Colony Management in general, which is, That the direction of such part of those affairs as are properly matters of State and fall within the Kings Prerogative is almost intirely in the hands of the People. I chuse to explain it by the Instance of So. Carolina, because I have been more intimately accquainted with that. There being no established Fund, or any sum of money given annually for Indian Expences beforehand (which is the case everywhere), the Governour and Council dare not incur an Expence, upon any Occasion, without first consulting the Assembly if that be possible; who are often called on purpose, when the Indians make visits to the Government.[52] On pretence of judging of the Expediency of any expence, they send to the Governour for all Letters, and Papers, and Talks, for Information; Then they generally confer with the Council on the subject matter, and afterwards recommend minutely not only the very Presents to be given, and to what particular Indians by name, but every measure to be taken, and how; And sometimes they are present at Audiences. Their Journals are full of those things.[53] And when they vote any money for sending an Agent to either of the Nations, they take care at the

The King's Prerogative at present exercised by the Assemblies.

---

[52] The South Carolina Assembly complained that Indian expenses were a "great Burthen to the People [and] are daily increasing . . ." in a message to Governor James Glen on March 7, 1747. Glen answered that prices for Indian gifts were also increasing. See "Council Journals," Vol. XV (1747-1748), pp. 160, 179-81.

[53] See *ibid.*, pp. 316, 345-46, where the lower house asked for all papers relating to the Cherokee agency. The "Journals of the Commons House of Assembly" are, as Atkin says, filled with reports of committees on Indian affairs and deliberations concerning expenses "For Indians."

same time to recommend one among themselves[54] (tho' not the fittest) to be the Person; whom the Governours thereby find themselves obliged to approve of to avoid a misunderstanding. And I [have] known such appointed by them contrary to their declared Judgment; and recalled whenever the Assembly desired it.

I thought [this] long Introduction of Facts, tho' dry and tedious, yet necessary, to enable your Lordships to form the better Judgment, of what I propose to offer next for retrieving and establishing our Interest among the Indian Nations & consequently the future security of our Colonies.

Character of the Indians.

No people in the World understand and pursue their true National Interest, better than the Indians. How sanguinary soever they are towards their Enemies, from a misguided Passion of Heroism, and a love of their country; yet they are otherways truly humane, hospitable, and equitable. And how fraudulent soever they have been reputed, from the Appearance of their military Actions, in which according to their method of War, Glory cannot be accquired without Cunning & Stratagem; Yet in their publick Treaties no People on earth are more open, explicit, and Direct. Nor are they excelled by any in the observance of them. Witness in particular the Treaties of the five Nations with the Government of New York; in which there hath been no Breach yet on their Part, since 1609 at first under the Dutch, and since 1664 under the English. And so patient are the Indians in general under the abuses of our Traders, that so [22] numerous as the occasions have been for Complaint, I have never known an Instance in my time of a Complaint made, from either of the Nations in alliance with So. Carolina, against any particular Trader by name, with a view of punishing him by Removal. When they intended it, they have been easily pacified & prevented. It were easy to make appear, with respect to (I believe I may say) all Ruptures of Consequence between the Indians & the white People, and the Massacres that ensued, which have created such a Horror of the former, That the latter were first the Aggressors; the Indians being driven thereto under Oppressions and Abuses, and to vindicate their Natural Rights. [The early and long Series of Calamities and Distreses which Virginia Struggled under with them in its Infancy, was owing, (tho' no Historian hath made

N. B. This was left out.

---

[54] Confirmed by the house journals. James Bullock and James Maxwell were members of the lower house. *S.C. Assembly Journals*, 1741-42, pp. 53, 330, 337.

the Observation) to Sr. Richd Grenville's burning an Indian Town and Destroying their Corn in 1585, after a very hospitable Reception, in revenge for a Silver Cup stolen by an Indian, who did not know the difference of Value between that and a horn Spoon; which could not but shock their natural Ideas of Equity— The great Massacre committed by the Yamasee Indians in So. Carolina in 1715[55] was owing to the continued Oppressions and ill Usage they received from a publick Agent; of which they often Complained in vain; being such that their King told a Person from whom I had it, they could bear them no longer. But they were so unwilling to come to that Extremity, and there was [so] little Treachery in their Execution of it, that they declared beforehand not only their Intention, but named the very day, which was treated with Slight, till it was too late— The great Massacre committed by the Natchez Indians upon the French on the Missisippi River in 1729 was certainly owing to the Obstruction which the French gave to their Trading with the English.[56] Le Pere Charlevoix[57] owns, that M. de Chepar, who commanded the Post in that Nation was (un peu brouille) a little embroiled with them, without telling the Reason. But he could not conceal, that they were hurried into striking the Blow sooner than the day appointed, upon hearing that 120 Horses loaded with English Goods were enter'd into [their] Country— The Blow also which was struck upon the French by the Chactaw Indians in 1746 was owing to the French not permitting them to have a free Trade with the English, when that Nation was almost Naked, and the French themselves were unable to supply them with Necessaries.][58] The policy of the Indians is Simple and **Their Policy** Plain. Tis confined to the Securing their personal Safety, a Supply of their Wants, and fair Usage. As we are the best able to supply all their wants, and on the easiest terms, they know it

---

[55] See note 24 for causes of this war.

[56] Confirmed in John R. Swanton, *Early History of the Creek Indians and Their Neighbors* (Washington, D. C., 1922), p. 416. The French claimed the British traders were responsible. See *ibid. Adair's History*, p. 379, mentions the influence of British traders and the Chickasaw.

[57] Pierre François Xavier de Charlevoix (1682-1761), French explorer and historian, was a traveller in New France in the 1720's and recorded his experiences in his *Journal historique*. He is also the author of *Histoire de la Nouvelle France* (1744). He was accurate, according to the standards of his day, but his works should be used with caution.

[58] Brackets are in the MS. For an elaboration of the causes of the revolt of the Choctaw, see Atkin, "Choctaw Revolt"; *Adair's History*, p. 353 ff.

The best Means
to be used
with them.

to be their true Interest to stick close to us, provided we shew an equal Regard also with the French, to their Safety and good usage. We have nothing therefore left to do, the Ballance being in our own hands, but, with the continuance of the same Trade as we now carry on with them, to Build Forts (not by Surprize, and against their will, as the French do but) for their sakes as well as our own, in such Nations as are or shall be desirous of it; To practice therein the same little ingratiating Arts as the French do; and above all, to begin with building Forts in their hearts, that is, *to put the Trade and Traders first under a good Regulation*; after which we may build Forts wherever we please. No Politicks whatever will be able to gain the affections of the Indians from us; nor anything but Conquest by superior Force, drive us out of their Countries. And if we can but once confine the French to the lakes of Canada and the Missisippi, we shall have nothing to envy them in North America.

The Colonies
cannot join in
regulating the
Trade.

There is not the least room to expect that our several Colonies, not united under any head, will or can joyn in making one general Regulation of the Trade. Much less I think can it be imagined, various as their Circumstances & Interests are, that they ever will agree among themselves upon a Joint Expence for the Service of the whole. They will be too apt to be content still, with defending each it's own actual Settlements and Plantations, as well as they can. Yet something farther they ought, and I dare say are willing to do for their Posterity; and something they may reasonably expect from the Mother Country for her own sake— Nor are Governours of the Colonies fit Persons to take the management of Indian Affairs, much less of a general regulation for the whole. By the frequent Changes of Governours, they are often intire Strangers to those sort of affairs, and not always open to advice. Being remote from the Indian Countries, they are obliged to act mostly by the Intelligence and Information of the Interested Traders, and having enough to do in mind the Provincial Affairs under their respective Charge, they are unable to go into the Indian Countries, and look into or conduct things themselves— A General Regulation therefore of the Indian Trade, obligatory upon all the Colonies, can be formed and take place only by Authority of Parliment. And the Direction of the Indian Affairs I humbly conceive, ought to be taken into his Majesty's own hands, and executed under his Royal Instructions, by Persons who must devote their whole Thoughts and Time to them, wherever it shall be Necessary. The Care and Superintendency of the general Welfare and Se-

Governours
not fit Persons
to undertake the
Management

a General
Regulation to be
made only by
the Parliament
&
executed under
the Royal
Direction.

curity of all the Colonies together, is truly a Royal Object, the Honour and Grandure of the Crown being [23] concerned therein. And all Negotiations and Treaties with Nations of Indians, as they do of right belong to, so they may not be thought unworthy of his Majesty's [own] Attention.

All the Indians with whom our Colonies have any Connection at present in North America, may be considered under two Divisions. In the first are to be comprehended, from Nova Scotia to Virginia inclusive, the Five, or as they have been latterly called, the Six Nations (Mohawks, Sennikas, Onondagas, Oneydoes, Cayugas, and Tuscaroras,)[59] next to N. York, with their Dependents (the Susquehannas, Delawars, Shawanoes, and other Tribes) on the back part of Virginia, Maryland & Pensylvania; and the Indians bordering on New England, commonly called, in regard I suppose to those others, the Eastern Nations. The latter are not allowed to exceed the Number of three hundred. . . . fighting Men........................300
For tho the whole number of the different Tribes, so far as the extreme Eastern End of Nova Scotia is computed to be Eight hundred; yet Five hundred thereof are said to be professedly in the French Interest —The *Six Nations* according to the largest and best Accts, including those from the several Nations, who either from Discontent at home, or to have a new Hunting Ground, or for other Reasons, are settled on the Ohio River, do not exceed Fifteen hundred Men[60]...............1500
who are the Lords Paramount of the red Complexion; united in a League immemorial, like that of the United Provinces of the Netherlands; the Consent of the whole being necessary in all Publick Deliborations by their Sachems in a General Council. Their Character and great Influence even on remote Nations is universally known.—The *Susquahannahs* their Dependants on the River of that name and Westward, are commonly reputed Six hundred Men....................................600.
The *Delawares, Shawanoes* (or Savanoes) & *other small Tribes* their Dependants also, on the River Ohio, (besides their own People there) are near Five Hundred Men...........500.
According to a particular Account taken Tribe by Tribe, and delivered by some of themselves in 1748, the number of the whole on that River, including the Colonies of the Six Nations,

[59] For the accepted spelling of these tribal names, see note 18.
[60] Sir William Johnson's estimate is slightly higher in 1763. *New York Colonial Documents,* VII, 582.

was then Seven hundred, eighty nine Men; (729) [789] among them were Twenty seven French Mohawks, mixed with the other Mohawks; which I suppose were sent thither by the French politically from near Montreal, where many from the Six Nations live, known by the name of Shawendadies and Cahnuagae [61] or praying Indians, who deserted their several Nations for various Reasons; But with whom the Six Nations still retain a great Influence—

The *Twightwees* [62] to the Westward near the Wabashe River, Number of the Nation, as well as of those in our Interest, unknown,..................................... ———

in all 2900

In the other Division may be comprehended all the rest of our friendly Indians, on the back of No. Carolina, & South Carolina and Georgia, Southward of the Hogohege or great Cherokee River, and Westward so far as the greater Missisippi River, into which that other falls, after its Junction with the Ohio and the Wabashe. Which Indians consist of several Nations, intirely independant of each other, to wit.

The Cherokees, commonly distinguished by the
    Names of Upper, Lower, & Middle above
    three Thousand Men................... 3000

The Catawbas but little more than Three hun-
    dred, perhaps Twenty [63]................. 320

[24] Brot over. 3320.

The Chicasaws, not more than Four hundred and
    Eighty in all places, to wit
    in the Nation .... 350 ⎫
    at their Camp on the borders of the upper
    Creek Nation .... 80 ⎬ 480.
    upon Savano River .... 50 ⎭

---

[61] Caughnawaga Mohawk living near Montreal.

[62] Or Miami. See the introduction for the account of the massacre at the Twightwee town of Pickawillany.

[63] Atkin's estimate agrees with that of Governor James Glen in Milling, *Colonial South Carolina: Two Contemporary Descriptions*, p. 68.

The Creeks, Lower Nation, living apart, and by some called Coweta's about Twelve hundred Men 1200
Upper Nation distinguish'd by the name of Tallapoosies Abecas, and Alibamas, (as by an acco. taken in [Novr] 1749) 1180
Savanoes, from the North, incorporated among those three Tribes................... 185

1365

2565.

Of the Alibamas four little Towns having 155 Men, next to & very near the French Fort, are intirely in the French Interest; as well as probably the Savanoes. But are all obliged to observe the same Terms with us, as the rest of the Nations.

————

6365.

The Chactaws, who in 1738 were first brought by Lt. Govr. Bull [64] to make a Treaty of Peace and Commerce with us in Charles Town, which was defeated by the murder of some of our Traders on the Path by some Young Chactaws employed by the French to waylay them; and who revolted from the French unable to supply them in 1746 during the late War & in April following made a second Treaty of Peace & Commerce with us in Charles Town by a solemn Embassy for that [purpose]; *being not duly supported* in their Extremities, after the lengths they had gone upon that Occasion, made a Peace again with the French; who having got some of our Traders killed by Rewards for their Scalps (since the Peace in Europe), none of them ventured into the Nation since 1750. Nay a Person employed in 1752 to carry some Presents to the Nation, having had one of his Men killed in the way, was obliged to return without delivering them. So that the Chactaws, whatever Friends we may have among them, are as a Nation lost to us at Present. Their

---

[64] William Bull (1683-1755) was lieutenant governor of South Carolina from 1737 to 1743 and was succeeded by James Glen.

Number according to a particular Account
Town by Town, transmitted by Monsr.
Vaudreuil Govr. of Louisiana, to the Count
De Maurepas, Secretary of State in France,
(and which being taken in the late War, is
now in my Hands) amounted then to Three
thousand Six hundred Men [65]............   3600

There are other Indians, nearer, and upon the side of the
Missisippi River, with whom a Trade was carried on from Carolina above 50 Years ago; but whose Numbers are now so reduced
as to be of little Account, and are not visited by our present
Traders. The principal ones are the *Chachoumas*,[66] about One
hundred and fifty Men, living near the Head of the Yasou
River,[67] about 60 Miles either from the Chactaw, or the Chicasaw Nation. They frequent the latter Nation (whom they pretty
much resemble) for the sake of our Goods yet are sometimes at
War with them. The *Natchees* surviving, who massacred the
French in 1729, are dispersed chiefly among our Friends, (except some that live near the Missisippi, not far from the Chicasaws.) About 50 of them were some Years in the upper Cherokee
Nation, where taking Umbrage in 1746, at the Intercourse with
the French and their Indians, some [25] of them came with
their Families to Charles Town, and obtained leave for their
Security to live with others of their Nation in the Settlements.
And these with about fifteen [*hundred*] *Yamasoes* [68] at most,
living by St. Augustine (being the remainder of that Nation
which commenced the Indian War in 1715) are all the Indians
within the last mentioned Tract of Country; besides the
Floridans, dependant on the Spaniards, whose number is as little
[known] as themselves and their Country. As they never go
without the limits of Cape Florida, nor have any Intercourse
with either the white People, or other Indians of the continent,
they are by the nature of their Situation as detached therefrom,
as if they lived remote upon an Island.

I have taken no particular Notice of the few Remains in our
Several Colonies, of the *Ancient Natives* and Posessers of those

---

[65] Atkin's figures show reasonable correlation with those of James Glen
in *ibid.*, pp. 68-69.

[66] The Chakchiuma Indians. Population confirmed in John R. Swanton,
The Indians of Southeastern United States (Washington, D. C., 1946),
p. 107.

[67] The Yazoo River.

[68] The Yamasee Indians. Note that Atkin deleted the word *hundred*.

Territories, still living in our Settlements among the plantations. I think they cannot in the whole much exceed *four hundred Men*. And the chief Service they are of, is in hunting Game, destroying Vermin, and Beasts of Prey, and catching Runaway Slaves.

Before I proceed further, it will be necessary for forming a compleat Judgment of what I am about to propose, to give some account of the particular Situation, Character, and Disposition, severally of the aforesaid Nations that have made Treaties with the Government of So. Carolina. I shall take them in the order they lie from Charles Town—

Acco. of the
Situation
Character, &
Disposition of
the Southern
Nations.

The Chicasaws on Savano River, who left their Nation many Years since, had a Tract of about twenty thousand Acres of exeeding good Land, set apart for their use by that Government, upon Horse Creek just above Fort Moore, and partly opposite to where Fort Augusta now stands; almost due West from Charles Town about one hundred and fifty Miles; being at that time the extreme Western Frontier to our settlements in those parts. Since the settlement of Georgia, they have made but little real use of that Land; rambling between the two provinces. So that many of our People from an opinion of their absolute Right to it, and that a Title to Land derived from Indians is a sufficient one, independant of the crown, have made a practice of buying peices of that Tract with Punch and Rum it being so rich and Fertile as to produce 50 Bushels of Corn to an Acre, and is equally adapted for Wheat— Those Indians are not less brave, or less good Hunters than the Nation they came from (of which I shall speak presently); altho from the great Ease wherewith they accquire all necessaries, and too much Liquor ever at hand, they have been much Debauched. The Constant and too great Familiarity added thereto, which they have been used to among the Settlers, and the many Indian Traders daily in that Neighbourhood, hath made them somewhat Insolent and mischevious; insomuch that the Inhabitants thereabouts have been often terrified and put under Alarm. Which Evil cannot but increase, in proportion as the Settlements in Georgia extend more Westerly, as they undoubtedly now will as the Government of that Province is taken into his Majesty's own hands. So that those Indians in their present Situation, are of much more Disservice and will be daily more so, than of advantage. A great part of them did remove voluntarily to the River Ogechee, about the middle of Georgia; but returned, as I believe, by the persuasion of our Traders. Their chief connection is with the Lower Creeks, with whom they have always preserved a Friendship; and some of them have taken wives among the lower Cherokees; altho they have been at times at War with them. So that not much more than 30 Men remain in their old Habitations, about Fort Moore and Fort Augusta. Their King or Chief named Squirrel,[69] is reputed to have killed more Men with his own Hands, than any other Indian on the continent. And he hath [26] more Personal Weight and Authority than any other; his talks being listned to attentively by other Nations as well as his own. He was the Man that opened the Indian War in 1715. And he was very near doing the same again in 1744, being then disgusted, and having sent Runners to the other Nations with a painted War Stick, which was embraced. But by the measures pursued, the intended Rupture was prevented from taking Effect intirely; after Steps had been taken towards it, within the very Settlements. He hath been heard to say; That it was a thing indifferent to him where he lived; and that he had an Invitation from the Spaniards, with whom he had a Sister among the Yamasees.

Catawbas
their situation

The Catawbas are situated about Two hundred and ten Miles N.N.W. from Charles Town on the Wateree River (near its head), which falls into the River Santee. That was some Years ago a very fit post for them, to cover the So. Carolina Settlements on that side. But of late Years abundance of People, besides the new Comers from Europe, have been induced by the extraordinary goodness of the Land and the Kindness of the Climate in those parts, to remove from the back settlements of the Northern Colonies, and settle thereabout; insomuch that those Indians are now in a fair way to be surrounded by White People. The Government of So. Carolina hath indeed restrained the making surveys of Land within 30 Miles of them. But the surveyors of No. Carolina, imagining them to be within the bounds of that Province, have lately run lines by Chain thro' their very Towns, which must make them uneasy; and will cer-

---

[69] Leader of a band of Chickasaw settled near Fort Moore. See *ibid.*, pp. 117-18. The Squirrel presented a head of ". . . a Spanish Indian to the General [James Oglethorpe during the Saint Augustine campaign of 1740] who refused to receive it, calling it Barbarity. And that their King, the Squirrel, was very much disgusted, saying that it was the first Head he had brought him, and that it should be the last. And that if he was to carry one of our Heads to the Governour of Augustine he should have been used by him like a Man, as he had been now used by the General like a Dog." *S.C. Assembly Journals, 1741-1742*, p. 201.

tainly end in determining them at least to remove. For on account of the difference of manners and way of life, as well as the Damage done by stocks of [livestock] Creatures to their Crops of Provision on the Ground, and the unkind Treatment of our common People, besides the making Deer scarce when they interfere, Indians generally chuse to withdraw, as white People draw near to them— The Catawbas having by means of their situation never (tho' tamper'd with at a Distance) had any intercourse with the French, or Spaniards, are the most to be relied on of any of the Indians. They have ever proved faithful, [having] assisted us to subdue the Tuskaroroes in 1713; and [*having*] stuck to us in the Indian War in 1715;[70] And discovered to us a proposal made to them by the Cherokee to joyn in a War against us in 1733; and also a League formed by the management of the French in 1745 between their and our Indians (in which the lower Cherokees were the chief Actors) to break out War with us, to which they were invited, but refused to joyn. By such their Fidelity they have drawn on themselves the Ill will in particular of the Tuskaroroes, Savanoes, and Cherokees; and the hatred of the French, who incite their Indians to Harrass them; and for which the Catawbas have conceived a great aversion to the French. They are remarkably acute, and have a Principle, which it is our Interest to Cultivate. "That all Indians who have their supplies from, and are Friends to the English, should be Friends also to each other." As they make known all their Complaints of others unto, so they are directed intirely by the Government of So. Carolina. In War, they are inferior [to] no Indians whatever. The greatest loss perhaps the Six Nations ever Received at one time in Fight with Indians, was by them. Such is the Honour in Indian Estimation to be accquired by Killing any of them, that Indians as far remote as the Lakes go in quest of them. I have heard them reckon up Eleven different Nations, as well in the English as the French Interest, who were at War with them at one time; and almost all of whom first come through the Country of the Cherokees; who, the Catawbas complain, not only permit it, but assist them with Necessaries, & sometimes Guides. They are unwilling to make so numerous a Nation their declared Enemies, added to so many others; and the [27] rather as being our Friends. For the same Reason, they have chosen to obtain Satisfaction from

---

[70] Some Catawba participated in this war. Swanton, *The Indians of Southeastern United States*, p. 77.

the Savano River Chicasaws for some Hostilities, by the mediation of the Government of So. Carolina. Yet such is their
Magnanimity under those Circumstances, exposed as they are
without any proper place of Defence and Security, that in the
Year 1748, when the lower Cherokees of the Town of Keowee,
protected against our Traders some of the French Indians, who
carried off Mr. Haig [71] a Justice of the Peace, and another
Person with him, through that Nation to the French Settlements,
they said, "They had born with the ill usuage they had received
from the Cherokees on their Account, as it was the Governours
Desire; but that they hoped he would give them leave to take satisfaction from them for their Ill us[u]age of the white People."
And it was in Compliance only with the repeated Persuasions of
the So. Carolina Government, and the Invitation of that of N.
York, that they at last consented to send Deputies to a meeting
at Albany, to make Peace with the Six Nations; which they did
in 1751. Finding themselves gradually decreasing in Number,
and unable forever to withstand so many Nations, single, and
unassisted, without a Fort, and having scarce time for Hunting
enough to buy Necessaries, they had in a manner resolved to
remove, at first to Virginia, but afterwards had a mind to live
with or near the lower Creek Nation, who are well inclined
towards them—

Cherokees
their Situation

The Cherokees are situated from three hundred to four hundred & fifty miles N.W. from Charles Town; the first Town in
the lower Settlements or Nation, on this side the Mountains,
being three hundred miles from thence, and it is about one hundred and fifty Miles across or through the middle Settlements
in the intermediate Vallies, to the last Town in the upper nation or Settlements on the other side of the Mountains; From
whence it is near the same Distance to Williamsburgh in Virginia, that it is to Charles Town— This is a most important
Country by it's nature and Situation, lying in a very extraordinary and remarkable manner among the Mountains in the
midst of the Heads of several large Rivers, that have Communication with different and remote parts on all sides; to wit, the
Savano and other Rivers, that flow Eastward into the Atlantick
Ocean; the Chatahuchee and Flint Rivers, that uniting near

---

[71] George Haig was a prominent back-country Carolinian who engaged
in Indian trade, land purchases, and surveying. He was taken prisoner by
the Indians and later killed. See Meriwether, *Expansion of South Carolina*,
pp. 58-59; *Adair's History*, p. 369.

49

Apalatchee flow Southward into the Gulph of Mexico; and the Branches of the Hogohege or great Cherokee River, that flows westward into the Missisippi, and is joined by the Ohio River that hath its source northerly so far as Lake Erie, and the Country of the Sennekas, to which there is a Straiter and more direct Passage from the Cherokee Towns, by very short and easy Transitions from one Stream to another of the numerous Branches of the Ohio nearest to the back of Virginia, Maryland, and Pensylvania. The high ridge of Mountains which runs behind them N.E. and S.W., continues on the back of No. Carolina a due westerly course from the Cherokees, parralel with the Hogohege River; there being no Mountains whatever to the Southward of the lower Cherokee Towns near the Latitude of 34, as is represented in almost all Maps. From the lower to the upper Towns, the passage through the Mountains is so narrow, that two Horses can scarce go abreast. So that the Cherokee Country is the best formed by Nature, for the dominion of the Inland Indian Nations on this side of the Missisippi and the Lakes. From the numerous Appearances of a variety and plenty of Ores, it is not improbable that great Treasures may be contained in the Mountains— The Cherokees are the most Ingenious Indians, of which their Baskets and Carpets are Instances. But they are far less Warlike than either the Catawbas, Chicasaws, or Creeks. The upper and lower Cherokees differ from each other, as much almost as two different Nations. The upper (among whom the Emperor resides) being much more warlike, better Governed, better affected to us, and as sober and well behaved as the others are debauched and Insolent, for the [28] Reasons before given. They seldom take part even in each others Wars; which is the case also with the upper and lower Creeks, with whom they are often at War; that is the Lower Cherokees, with the lower Creeks. When the upper and lower of both Nations engage in a War, the Lower Cherokees whose Towns being the most and Nearest [are much exposed], are glad to accept the Mediation of the So. Carolina Government, to make a Peace between them. The middle Cherokees, are much more like the upper, than the lower. Since the Cherokees sent Deputies to the Six Nations, and made a Peace with them (I think in 1742), they have been free from War with them, tho' not altogether with their Dependents. But they have underhand Encouraged and Promoted it against the Catawbas; and did even form a Confederacy with those of the Six Nations and others in the French Interest, to cut them off intirely. And they have also endeavoured, to engage those Indians in their Interest against the Creeks. They are the only Indians among the Southern Nations, who have sent any of their Chiefs to England. In 1730 the then Emperor Moytoy, with the consent of the whole Nation at a general Meeting, sent six Deputies over, with the Crown of the Nation; which was laid, with the scalps of their Enemies &c at his Majesty's feet, in token of their Subjection and obedience. Articles of Friendship and Commerce were then proposed and agreed to, which were afterwards accepted and confirmed at another general meeting of the Nation. The Counterpart of which Articles Moytoys Son the present Emperour Ousteaika Shaleloske [72] hath since produced at different Interviews with the Government of So. Carolina, in token of his observance of them. One of the said Articles is, "That the Cherokees shall not trade with the white Men of any other Nation; nor Permit White Men of any other Nation to build any Forts, Cabins, or plant any Corn amongst 'em, or near to any of their Towns, or upon the Lands belonging to our King.[73] And if any such attempt shall be made, they are to accquaint the English Governo[u]r therewith, and to do whatever he directs in order to maintain & defend the King's Right to the Country of Carolina." This Article hath hitherto been punctually Complied with. In January 1745/6 the Emperour & head men of the upper nation sent notice to the Governour, "That they had just made a Peace with the Savanoes, who had come with two Frenchmen, and promised them a Peace with all the Indians round them. That those Frenchmen proposed to come again the next September, with Savanoes, Illinois, and others, in all Six Nations; and talked of nothing but Peace of which they the Cherokees [sent] Word, lest they should prove Rogues and Spies; that he might provide against their attempts." With a grant of the Ammunition they desired on that occasion, to defend themselves against their and our Enemies, an assurance was given of further Assistance in case they should be Disturbed by

---

[72] Atkin probably refers to the Cherokee chief "Autossity Ustonecka," "Indian Books of South Carolina," Vol. V, p. 109. He was also known as Outacite. A print of him appears in Chapman J. Milling, *Red Carolinians* (Chapel Hill, N. C., 1940), p. 342. Outacity, or Man Killer, was a title given a seasoned Cherokee war chief. See *ibid.*, p. 29. This chief was one of three Cherokee leaders who visited London in 1762. See illustration facing this page.

[73] Confirmed by Crane, *Southern Frontier*, pp. 299-300.

THREE CHEROKEE CHIEFS WHO VISITED LONDON IN 1762

The title of the print, from a painting by Sir Joshua Reynolds, reads: *"The three Cherokees. came over from the head of the River Savanna to London, 1762. 1. Their Interpreter that was Poisoned. 2. Outacite or Man-Killer; who Sets up the War Whoop, as,* (Woach Woach ha ha hoch Waoch) *with his Wampum. 3. Austenaco or King, a great Warrior who has his Calumet or Pipe, by taking a Whiff of which, is their most Sacred emblem of Peace. 4. Uschesees y Great Hunter. or Scalpper, as the Character of a Warrior depends on the Number of Scalps, he has them without Number:"* The Indians were escorted by Lieutenant Henry Timberlake, and their interpreter died en route to London. Alden, *John Stuart,* p. 133.

(Courtesy Bureau of American Ethnology and the British Museum)

the French. In the said September, not having received the Ammunition promised, they gave it as a Reason for not opposing the coming of the French and their Indians into their Towns, as they were prepared to do, the middle and even some of the lower Cherokees having offered their Assistance. They then agreed to a Peace with the French and all their Indians, under the Negotiation of a Frenchman (in appearance of some consequence) who came with a large Body of Savanoes (or Shawanoes), Nottawagas,[74] and others, while a Body of French and Indians were within Six Days Journey; and whom they suffered to set up the French Colours in the mother Town Chotee. But they sent word at the same time to the Governour "That their Mouths and looks only, & not their Hearts, accepted the Peace." [29] And when an Agent for the Province got thither on that Occasion, they frankly acknowledged "That they were afraid of the French and their Indians, who were great Warriors & Numerous; being unable of themselves to withstand them, not having [any] place to defend their Wives and Children which they desired might be considered; and earnestly begged, that we would build two Forts in their Towns (upper Towns) for the protection of their Families, and to enable them to keep out the French, who they beleived else would force themselves upon them. That they wanted nothing for the Land, it being already all our own; and would give an assistance in their Power, and supply the Garrison with Provisions for Two Years; Urging that if we would build such Forts among them, every thing would then be as we pleased, whereas if we let the French take a Footing first among them, then every thing would be as they pleased." Being threatened Year after Year with an Army of French Men and Indians coming to those upper Towns, they have continued to implore our Assistance, and importuned the Governor to build at least one Fort for them. It hath been repeatedly promised. And they have complained from time to time of the breach of that Promise. The lower Cherokees indeed (that is a great part of them) are of another Disposition; arising from different Causes. I have mentioned before such part as is owing to the Irregularities and Disorders introduced by our Traders, and chiefly by the means of Rum. The rest is owing to the Intrigues of the French. As they have long had their eyes

---

[74] The Nottaway of the Iroquoian linguistic family. They lived along the river of the same name in southeastern Virginia. John R. Swanton, *The Indian Tribes of North America* (Washington, D.C., 1952), p. 65.

upon the Cherokee Country, they have taken different ways with those Indians in order to succeed. They sent presents to the upper and lower Towns to engage their Friendship, by the hands of such Indians of the Six Nations (being in Alliance with the Cherokees) as were in their Interest. The Frenchmen who treated in Person with the upper Cherokees, pretended to want only a Peace or Liberty for their Boats to pass up[*p*] and down the Rivers unmolested; that they came to be near them, and would sell them Goods cheaper than the English, mentioning some unheard of Rates. The two Head Men of the lower Cherokees, who as I said before were in England in 1730, and having been carried Prisoners to Canada, where they lived some Years, and were made Great Men, were employd as Emissaries to the Cherokees (For according to the Custom of Indians, Prisoners being adopted become of the same Nation with the Captors); those Men Harrangued through the Nation in praise of the better usage by the French than the English, and the greater plenty of Ammunition among them; and persuaded some of their Countrymen to go with them and see the French. The Savanoes (or Shawanoes) and Nottawagas, who frequented the Nation, danced and regaled continually with the mad Young Cherokees in the lower Towns, endeavouring to lead them into a Rupture with us, by telling them of the great Number of French and Indians coming to the upper Towns, & persuading them to fall upon the white people in our Settlements; and if the White People proved too hard for them, then to remove and live with them. The Nottowagas having led the way by entering into the Settlements and carrying off (as beforemention'd) Mr. Haig a Justice of the Peace, and one Mr. Brown [75] (whom they said they borrowed to talk with their White Men in the French Towns), and no Satisfaction being exacted from the People of Keowee Town for the Protection they gave some of those Indians against some of our Traders and Friends [30] of a Neighbouring Town, who attempted to stop them; nor from that or any of the other lower Towns, for the abuses and Violences offered to our Traders, and a formal proposal on that occasion to kill all our Traders, tho' the upper and middle Cherokees interested themselves greatly in our Favour; those Lower Cherokees conceiving a Contempt of our People, some of

---

[75] The half-breed son of Thomas Brown, prominent Catawba trader of the 1730's. Meriwether, *Expansion of South Carolina*, pp. 58-59; *Adair's History*, p. 369.

them were induced at last, to go privately into the settlements along with the Savanoes and Nottowagas, who with the Tawes, Nantouyas, and other French Indians (with a view to create a Difference between us and the Cherokees) made a Practice Year after Year of killing and carrying away through the Cherokee Nations, not only our Settlement Indians, but half breed Slaves, Mulattoes, and Mustees; and killed several white People; and even went in quest of Colonel Pawley,[76] and Capt. Fairchild [77] who had attended him as Agent. Many Traders were killed from time to time in the Nation, some of them undoubtedly by the Cherokees themselves of the lower Towns, and their Goods plundered by them. And they were restrained from striking one general Blow, by the Prudence of the upper and middle Cherokees, and a few among themselves. The Trade being at last stopt for a time, in order to obtain Satisfaction, some of them went to Virginia to get Traders; But not succeeding intirely, and being pushed hard in War by the Creeks, the People of several lower Towns fled over the Mountains, among them the Keowees, the Satisfaction demanded having never been obtained. And having at first talked of removing to live with the Nottowegas, some Cherokees went in 1752 to the lower Shawnoes Town on the Ohio, and accquainted them that 1400 of their People intended to come and live among them, being unable to stay in their own Country under the anger of the English. This would have very bad Consequences, as we should lose the best Security we now have for their Behaviour; by their Remoteness at present from French supplies. The upper Cherokees are really to be pitied. They acknowledge that they cannot do without us. But are not in Condition to act in regard to the Northern Indians according to their Inclination. They lament that by a stop being put to the Trade, the innocent part of the Nation suffer alike with the Guilty. And being perplexed in relation to the People of the Six Nations, whom they find divided in their Attachment to the English and the French, they say very truly, that we ourselves made the Peace for them with those Nations.

---

[76] Colonel George Pawley was the agent who made the important land purchase from the Cherokee at Ninety-Six on the Cherokee trail from Charleston to Keowee. The purchase took place in 1746. See the discussion concerning Pawley's report in the "Journals of the Commons House of Assembly," Vol. XXII (1746-1747), pp. 478-79, 483-84, 489. Also see Meriwether, *Expansion of South Carolina*, pp. 194-95.

[77] Captain John Fairchild was a South Carolina surveyor, ranger captain, and frontier land-owner in the 1740's and 1750's. See *ibid.*, pp. 60, 62, 64, 103.

54

In order to put a stop to the Inroads of the French Indians through the Cherokee Nation, and to protect the back Settlers in So. Carolina against the Insults before mentioned, it was judged absolutely necessary by the Council and Assembly from time to time from April 1747, to build a Fort in one of the lower Cherokee Towns. In May, 1752 £3000 Current money was voted the last time, for building that Fort near Keowee (the first Town going from Charles Town & the principal Rendezvous of the Northern Indians) with the partial consideration, in regard to the uncertain Limits of Georgia, of placing it within the undoubted limits of that Province. Whereas it might be so placed, as to answer not only the same, but other Purposes also. Accordingly in Novr. 1753 a Fort [78] was built under the Governour's [79] Direction & Inspection, on this side Keowee River, opposite to and within Gun Shot of that Town; which was then Deserted. The Sufficiency of it may be judged of from hence, that it was begun & ended in twenty two Days, being a square of about a Quarter of an Acre, flanked with four Bastions, the Rampart of Earth about Six Feet High, surrounded with a Ditch five feet deep and twelve Broad, covered with Pallisadoes in the front of each Curtain, and in which a Sergeant and fourteen Men were left as a Garrison; who are not qualified to go in Pursuit of any Indians; nor are the Indians obliged to go by it. Indeed the Governour [31] in a Message to the Assembly said, it was necessary, to enforce new Regulations and to keep our Traders in awe.

Lower Creeks their Situation

The Creeks are situated from W.N.W. to W.S.W. from Charles Town upon different Rivers to wit. The *Lower Nation* are about Three hundred & Seventy Miles from Charles Town (that is either of their two First Towns, Chatahuchee, or Coweta), upon the Western Bank of the Chatahuchee River, near the middle of its Course. Which taking its Rise as before mentioned, among the Western lower Cherokee Towns, runs southwest, and then Southerly; and after being joined near Apalatchee by Flint River, which takes its rise to the Eastward near some of the same Towns, emptys itself into the Gulf of Mexico, near the Bay of Apalatchee, being heretofore called Apalachicola River. There are no Creek Towns below the said Fork; which is Distant about 60 or 70 Miles by Land from the Sea. This is

[78] Fort Prince George.
[79] Governor James Glen.

THE
REPORT

Anecdotes con-
cerning the same
with regard to
the French.

a most delightfull River in all its known Parts, watering an uninhabited Country to the Eastward, especially in Apalatchee towards the Sea Coast inferior to none that is known, in richness
and Fertility of Soil. One Capt. Ellis, who served as a Pilot
under General Perrier Governor of Louisiana,[80] when he surveyed that Coast by order of the French King, told me, That
he found three fathom and a half at Low Water upon the Bar;
and that the Water was fresh out at sea some Leagues off. This
River, which is infinitely the best that flows on this side the
Missisippi into the Gulf of Mexico, and to us is of more real
Value perhaps than the Missisippi itself would be (for that besides being so remote, is extremely rapid, choaked at the mouth
with Flats, its Navigation very Dangerous, and Air unhealthy in
the lower Parts); I say this River is of the greatest Importance
either to the English or to the French, to be possessed of the
command thereof. Without it the French cannot possibly compleat their scheme of cutting us off from the Indian Nations
by a sort of Line of Forts on the back of all our Colonies from
Lake Erie to the Gulph of Mexico. And if they were possessed
of that River, the Communication between their Settlements
from North to South throughout would become vastly shorter
and safer. And they would also be able to convey supplies of
Goods to the Cherokees easily, which at present is the Principal difficulty they labour under. They have certainly had their
Eye upon that Country for a long time; and discovered a
Jealousy of us (who have always had Traders Resident in most
of the Creek Towns) so long [ago] as in 1733, when the first
Settlers of Georgia [arrived]. For at that time, as the said
Capt. Ellis told me, Monsr. Bienville [81] who then Succeeded
General Perrier as Governour of Louisiana, not comprehending
what was meant by Georgia, and fearing it was the Country of
Apalatchee, sent a Vessel to the mouth of the Chatahuchee River,
on purpose to reconnoitre. The next Governour Mons. Vaudreüil,
in a Letter dated in February 1743/4 to the French Secretary
of State, proposed, (as I mentioned above) to penetrate into the
Lower Creek Towns on that River and in 1750 some Officers

---

[80] M. Perrier (Périer or Sieur Perrier) de Salvert was governor of
Louisiana from 1726 to 1733. He led the victorious campaign against the
Natchez in 1730-1731. See *New York Colonial Documents,* IX, 1025;
Justin Winsor, *Narrative and Critical History of America* (New York,
1887), V, 46.

[81] Jean Baptiste Lemoyne, Sieur de Bienville (1680-1768) aided his
older brother Iberville in the founding of Louisiana. Jean was governor
from 1718 to 1724 and from 1733 to 1743.

THE
REPORT

&
important
Advantages to be
reaped by the
Possession of
the Chattahuchee
River.

and Men, having an Engineer among them, were sent from the Alibama Fort to the principal Town Coweta; where they set up the French Colours during their Stay. As to the importance of the Chatahuchee River to the English; it might be made to serve as a natural Boundary or Barrier from North to South, between the settlements of South Carolina and Georgia, and the western Nations of Indians; as well as to check the progress of the French Settlements in Louisiana Eastward. In this light it hath not at all been attended to by the Government of So. Carolina, which never attempted, or appeared desirous to fix a Fort upon some part of it; For no other reason, (seeing they might have done it long ago), but because the French had not yet attempted to do it; or advanced further than the upper Creeks. The Possession of the mouth of this River would give us a Port, where we now have none, in the Bay of Mexico; wherein Ships would lie in fresh Water free from Worm, and free from Hurricanes, which have been felt thereabouts. And from whence the Kings Ships at Jamaica, might upon occasion [32] have more ready supplies of Masts and other Naval Stores, and Provisions. And a beneficial Commerce might be also open'd with the Spaniards for Provisions &c, from whom the French at New Orleans now draw a considerable Sum in Specie. And in time of War, it might be a fit Port to cruise to advantage either upon the French or Spanish Ships, or to receive our own. Most of these last apparent Advantages have been thought of; and the fine Climate, & richness of Land, have helped to induce some Persons to wish for a Settlement to be made there immediately. And indeed we have an equitable Pretension to do it; because the Carolinians under Colonel Moore,[82] in 1703 in Queen Anns War, with the Assistance of the Creeks, made a compleat Conquest of the whole Country of Apalatchee, after a decisive Battle fought with the Spaniards and those Indians; every Town and Fort submitting that had not before been taken, and almost all the Natives but what were destroyed being Transported to the River Savano. In which State that Country continued at the Treaty of Utrecht, and since; free from any Possessor, till the Spaniards built a small Fort named St. Marks, on the Eastern side of the River Apalatchee in the bottom of

---

[82] James Moore (d. 1706) was governor of Carolina from 1700 to 1703. He was a planter, trader, and slave dealer, and besieged the town of Saint Augustine in Queen Anne's War. He also led an army of whites and Indians against the Apalachee in 1704. Crane, *Southern Frontier*, pp. 75 ff.

that Bay, for the sake of keeping a Communication between St. Augustine and Pansicola. But how desirable soever it is to take possession of the mouth of the River Chatahuchee, and to make a Settlement there, for my own part I must own, I think it scarce prudent Yet to attempt it openly, as being premature, until we can be sure of the Consent and Support of the Lower Creeks; [who, when on the commencement of the Indian War with us in 1715 they deserted all their habitations on the Branches of the River Alatamaha, and on Ogeehee River, as did the Apalatchees & Palachucolaes or Apalatchicolaes with others, theirs on the River Savano, retreated all together to the Chatahuchee, and incorporated there; the Apalatchicolaes, who were the Ancient Possessors, seating themselves lowest in the Fort made by the Flint River.] [83] For the Spaniards and French from different motives, will certainly concur heartily in opposing such an attempt. Nor can we in the present situation of things promise ourselves therein the Countenance of those Lower Creeks, who have given the People of Georgia so much uneasiness on Account of their Settlements even to the Eastward of the Alatamaha River; and have strongly objected to any white people, other than the Traders, going further westward. Another advantage that might arise from our Possessing the mouth of Chatahuchee is, that it might be the means of opening by Boats a New Branch of Trade with the Indians of Cape Florida; who have no convenient Fort on the Atlantick Ocean, nor can they be come at by Land, living among the bays. 'Tis true they have lived hitherto in Friendship only with the Spaniards. But Captain Lampriere of So. Carolina, who commanded a Privateer in the late War, and careen'd his Vessel among those bays, told me that some of the Chiefs of those Indians were very desirous of going with him to Charles Town, in order to Treat for a Trade from thence; but that he declined carrying them, fearing lest he might be blamed on Account of the Expence that might accrue. But what makes the mouth of the Chatahuchee River of more importance than any thing else, and which I never heard taken Notice of, is yet the very thing from whence alone we may conceive Hopes, or rather be assured with prudent Management, not only of the Consent, but the Support of the Creeks. I mentioned above the superior Influence which the French have among the Indian Nations, by

[83] Brackets are in the manuscript. The John Mitchell map of 1755 calls this fort the "Cherokee-Leechee or Apalachiola Ft."

their Ability to furnish them with sufficient Supplies of Ammunition, by means of their Water Carriage; whereas our Traders being obliged to carry their Goods many hundred Miles upon Horses, consulting their greatest Proffit, only carry but scanty supplies of that heavy Article and of small Value. Monsr. Vaudreuil in his Letter to the French Secretary of State, mention'd under that Head, Says "That it is impossible for the English, let them do what they will, to furnish all the Nations (in those parts) with a Quarter part of the Ammunition they have need of." Now it is Evident, if we could introduce Goods at the Mouth of the Chatahuchee [33] River, Ammunition like all other things might be carried in Plenty by Water into the very Towns of the Lower Creeks and by means of a Branch of that River, to within a very few Miles of the upper Creek Towns; [upon the Next River; and also by the same River, almost into the Lower Cherokee Towns;] from whence by a very short and easy Land Carriage, being transferr'd through the streams which flow from that Nation, it may be carried by Water to very distant Parts. And if the Creeks should once see a plenty of ammunition thus brought to their Doors, and also cheaper than before as the Traders might very well tender it, their own Interest then would certainly determine them to support us in the Possession of the Mouth of the Chatahuchee River.

Upper Creeks their Situation

The Upper Creek Nation is situated further West from four hundred and thirty to four hundred and Eighty Miles from Charles Town, up and between the Tallapoosee (Locushatchee, or Ockfuskee) River and the Coosaw River; the Distance across being 50 Miles from Tallasee the first Town on the former, to Coosaw Town on the latter. Those Rivers taking their Rise in the Mountains, unite in the Alibama River, which running Southwesterly discharges itself into the Bay and harbour of Mobile a little to the Westward of the Spanish Settlement at Pansicola. The Bar being Shallow and Dangerous, that harbour is fit only for small Vessels. And the air is Sickly and unwholesome, to the Town and Garrison of Fort St. Lewis; and the Land about it Poor. But yet the Harbour is of great Importance to the French, as they have by means of different Rivers that fall into it, an easy Communication by Water, with several the most potent Indian Nations on this side the Missisippi. At the head of the Alibama River, in the Fork of the two other aforsed. Rivers, the French have a Fort named Tholouse, and commonly called the Alibama Fort; which upon the breaking out of the Indian War with Carolina in 1715, they immediately seized

Account of the French Fort in that Nation.

the Opportunity of Building where we had a Factory for 28 Years before, altho they had taken their first footing in Mobile Bay but in 1701. [84 Here it may not be amiss to mention an Anecdote or two, concerng the french manner of proceeding to compass their Ends in those parts. Captain Ellis beforementioned told me, That he conversed at Mobile with a Frenchman, who was with Mr. De la salle in the last Voyage he made in 1684/5 to discover the mouth of the Missisippi River; who told him, they met with an English Sloop trading with the Indians at Mobile, and that Mr. De la salle having regaled the People and made them Drunk, while he kept his own sober, afterwards put them all to Death. P. De Charlevoix in his Relation of that Voyage, says, that going along the Coast in sight of it, La salle often approached near the Land in order to discover what he was in search of; yet makes no mention of any place he touched at before he got to St. Bernard's Bay. But adds, that after he had passed the mouth of the Missisippi he would have gone back again, *upon some Ideas which Indians gave him*; without saying where he met with those Indians. And the same Charlevoix, in his Relation of M. d'Iberville's Voyage afterwards on the same account in 1699, Says, That anchoring by the East Point of Mobile River, he landed on an Island near it since called Isle Dauphine, but which he then named Isle Massacre, because he perceived there the Heads and Bones of about 60 Persons [which he judged to have been massacred;] together with several Utensils still intire— Another Transaction of the like kind, ought not to [be] buried in Oblivion. Charlevoix relates, "that the Sieur de la Loire being sent by the Governour of Louisiana in 1713 with Goods, to settle stores at the Nation of Natche[e]s, found some Englishmen there (where by the way our Traders carried on a Trade before any French Ship had ever enter'd the Missisippi), who came from Carolina to engage those Indians to make War upon other Nations, in order to bring away Captives; and who were even suspected by the French to be Intriguing against them. After which that La Loire having received [an] Order to detain the Officer of the English, who stayed there alone, carried him to Mobile; where he was regaled by the Commanding Officer, and then Permitted to return. That he went by way of Pansacola, where he was also very well received by the Govr. But [34] that being willing to get to Carolina by way of the Ali-

---

84 Bracket is in manuscript.

bamoes, he fell into the Hands of a Hunting Party of the Tomees, who scalp'd him." The Story thus disguised by Charlevoix, (or those from whom he had it) was really this. Mr. Hewse, a private Gentleman, who came from Wales to Carolina, being a Man of some Fortune, Learning, and Piety; made it his Business to Travel among the Indian Nations, from Motives of Curiosity and Religion. And after accquiring a competent knowledge of their Languages, he endeavoured to instill into them the Christian Principles. His Appearance joyned to the respect which the Indians paid him, gave the Jealous French much uneasiness. Having not the least pretence for detaining him at Mobile, they let him go. But after experiencing the French Civility, soon after he left that Place, he was killed in the Woods, in his way towards the Creeks, by some Indians employed for that Purpose. Charlevoix adds, "That he did not know what it was set the Indians at that time against the English, but that the greatest part declared themselves all at once against them." Intimating thereby, that the Death of Mr. Hewse was owing to the same cause. Whereas that was so far from being the case, the Indian War being not then Commenced, that the Creek Indians sent a Party to take Revenge for his Death in our behalf.] [85] The Fort at the Alibamoes, being on the edge of the Coosaw River, is pallisadoed, and Surrounded with a Ditch, not large, nor of much Strength. On the Landside of it, is a rising Ground upon a level, the Distance of 100 or 150 Yards; behind which is a Valley sufficient to contain an Army, which may approach without any hurt, near enough under that cover to throw shells into the Fort. The Woods are close to the houses without. The Garrison, which depends upon the Indians for their Necessaries, was generally but from 20 to 25 Men, having only two Carriage Guns and four Swivel Guns; 'til being alarmed with our Intention to attack it the beginning of 1747, the French reinforced it to 45 Men, with two peices of Cannon more, and otherways strengthened it. It is about 150 miles distant from Mobile by Land, and about twice as far by Water. In dry Season, the Boats, on account of Sand Bars in the River, cannot go up so far as the Fort, without having small Boats sent down to lighten them. No Boat can at any time go more

N. B. This was
left out.

---

[85] Bracket is in the manuscript. Price Hughes (d. 1715), a Welsh gentleman and explorer, planned to establish a Welsh colony. His schemes caused countermeasures on the part of the French, and, as Atkin states, he was killed by Indians after being released from imprisonment by the French at Mobile. Crane, *Southern Frontier*, pp. 99 ff.

than two Miles above the Fort, upon the Coosaw River; nor more than two Miles above Tuckabatchee,[86] on the Tallapoosee River; on account of Water falls in each. The Coosaw River is full of those Water Falls. This is a very favourable Circumstance for us, not only as it puts a stop to the French Water Carriage any further that way, but because it will contribute greatly to the Security of any Fort which we may hereafter build higher up, on, or between either of those Rivers, which take their rise in the Mountains which run along Westward, on the South side of the great Cherokee River, which is distant from the most Northern Creek Towns about 80 or 90 Miles. And what Streams may run part of that Distance into it, is yet unknown. For not only in our Present Maps, there is not a single Stream mark'd out belonging to that very large and long extended River, any-where to the Westward of those Streams whereon the Cherokee Towns are Situated (but only the general Course of the River; altho' all great Rivers are supplied on both sides in a long Course with small Streams). But I have never heard of any Englishman that ever did go down that River, further than a few miles below the Cherokee Towns. In that part of it almost due North [from], and nearest to the upper Creek Towns, is a *Water Fall*, which being mark'd for Information only, as a fit Place for a Fort and Factory, in the Map of Carolina, trans-mitted by Govr. Nicholson,[87] was injudiously publish'd in Mr. Popple's Map of the British Colonies.[88] Mr. Bellin [89] in his Maps, mark'd at that fall an English Fort and Post, as actually being there. But the French know better. At this place it is to be feared they will endeavour to fix a Fort, if they cannot succeed with the Cherokees in opening a Communication through their Nation. For this will Yeild the French a much [35] Shorter, Easier, and Safer Communication, through the upper Creek Nation, (with their Permission) than they have at present, from the Gulf of Mexico to the Ohio, Lake Erie, and the Illinois; without going up through the tedious and

of the Water Fall
in that part of the
great Cherokee
River nearest to
this Nation
&
the Importance
of its Possession
to the French.

86 Or Togobatche (Tukabatchi). An Upper Creek town on the west bank of the Tallapoosa River opposite modern Tallasse, Alabama.

87 Francis Nicholson (1655-1728) was governor of five colonies. His last assignment was South Carolina, 1720-1725. Crane, *Southern Frontier*, covers this administration.

88 Atkin probably refers to Henry Popple's *Map of the British Empire in America* . . . (London, 1732). See Winsor, *op. cit.*, V, 81, 235.

89 Jacques Nicolas Bellin (1703-1772), was a royal French engineer who made the maps published in Charlevoix's *Histoire de la Nouvelle France*. Winsor, *op. cit.*, IV, 358; V, 429.

Character of
the Creeks.
Upper & Lower

Dangerous Missisippi. And if this should be Effected, our Traders will be stopt from going any further Westward.

As to the Character and Disposition of the Creeks; They are the most refined and Political Indians, being very Speculative, Sensible, Discreet, Sober, well Governed by their Head Men; and withal by no means wanting Bravery. The Lower Creeks indeed fall short of the upper in some part of this Character; being far less Sober, and therefore not so orderly. Which is Occasioned by the great Quantities of Spirituous Liquors, carried by the Augusta Rum Traders to them being the nearest—

their Policy.

The Policy of the Creeks leads them to live in Peace with all their Neighbours; but above all to preserve a good Understanding with all white People, English, French, and Spaniards; with each of whom they have Intercourse. This last principle is frequently inculcated by some of the Chiefs in their Harrangues, from the motives of their National Safety and Interest, while they take part against neither, but are Courted by them Severally, and receive Presents from each. The same Principle was enforced by the dying charge of the Old Emperor Brim to his Son Malatchi, the Present Chief of the lower Nation, "never to suffer the Blood of any White Men to be spilt on his Ground." The Conduct of the Creeks conformable to those Principles (which was eminent during the last War) hath rendered them of Superior Weight among the Southern Nations, as holding the Ballance between their European Neighbours, and esteemed or feared by the rest of the red People—

Disposition toward
other Indians.

Notwithstanding the general Disposition of the Creeks to live in Peace with the Neighbouring Nations, they are often at War with the Cherokees, tho' the upper do not always take part with the Lower therein; as on the other hand, the upper Cherokees do not always take part with the lower. These two being the most numerous (the Chactaws excepted), are the contending Nations of the South. The Creeks have an old Grudge against the Cherokees, for joining the Carolina Army in the Indian War in 1715, and falling on them unexpectedly. The repeated losses they have sustained on each side since, have so imbittered their Minds, that it hath been found a very difficult matter to reconcile them. So that the Peace made between them from time to time, hath been of [no] long Duration, but soon followed by a Rupture. This under the present state of our Affairs among the Indians, hath been attended with lucky Consequences to Carolina, as it hath been the means of Disconcerting the Intrigues of the French. But whenever those affairs shall assume such a Change, that we may be intirely secure of both these Nations, it will then become a Point of great Moment, by any means possible to reconcile them effectually. The Creeks do also sometimes go against the Floridans, against whom they were incited heretofore by the Carolina Government; who after the Conquest of Apalatchee having destroyed some whole Tribes (the Timooquas [90] and Tacoboggas [91] next [to] St. Augustine and St. Marks), encouraged the Creeks to War upon those Indians, for the sake of making Slaves of them. By which means until the breaking out of the Indian War, a Slave Trade only was promoted in Florida; which drove those Indians to the extreme Parts of the Cape among the bays, leaving the finest part of their Country uninhabited; as it remains at this Day— The Creeks in general are well affected to the English, for the sake of our Goods, much better than to the Spaniards or [the] French. The Lower Creeks are not quite so well Affected to us, as the Upper. This hath been much admired at, [36] considering that the latter have a French Fort among them. But the real Reason is, that the abuses, disorderly Practices, and Evil Example of the Rum Dealers & other unlicensed Traders that frequent the lower Creeks, have produced in them a Contemptible Opinion of us; as the same Reasons have done among the Lower Cherokees. At the same time they see the Upper Creeks enjoying advantages by the French Fort, which they do not. And they have also for some time been displeased on Account of some Partiality shewn between them and the Cherokees. They have even said that, if they were to kill our Traders as the Cherokees had done, we should send for them in the like manner, and give them Presents— The Upper Creeks how much soever they prefer our Friendship to that of the French, yet in regard to the Fort at the Alibamaos, the Majority of their Nation (which is composed of different Tribes) countenance and favour it, on Account of their having their Guns mended there Gratis, and of their ancient leading Men receiving little Presents to supply their Necessities; which are Advantages they do not receive from us. The Alibama Towns are firmly attached to to it; for being all within 7 miles (Puckana Town [92] is adjoining), they not only partake of more of those

toward the English.

to the French Fort at the Alibamas.

---

[90] Timucua Indians.

[91] Tocobaga Indians of Timucuan affinity.

[92] Puckna was a former village of the Upper Creeks in what is now the southwest part of Clay county, Alabama. Hodge, *Handbook of the American Indians,* II, 315.

advantages, but in Exchange for Provisions have a full supply of Ammunition, in which the Men of that Garrison even Receive their Pay. The Cheifs of the Tallipoosie and Abeka Towns [93] the most in our Interest; are afraid openly to promote anything to its Prejudice against the Inclination of their People. Therefore they never would listen to any Proposal for taking it. The utmost they could be brought to, was to Consent that we

& to our building a Fort in the Upper Nation.

also might build a Fort amongst them. Which Consent the Lieutt Governour Mr. Bull prevailed on them to give in October 1743. In consequence whereof, a Pallisade Fort 150 Feet Square was begun by the Traders, according to the advice of those Chiefs, opposite to Ockfuskee Town on that River;[94] that place being Judged by them to be the most Convenient & Secure. It was finished (soon after the present Governour's Arrival) in March following. But there was never a Man sent into Garrison. In November 1746, some of their Chiefs being in Charles Town, were prevailed on again, as a Proof of their Friendship towards us, and for the Security of our Traders against the French during the War, to Consent to our Building a Fort at Muccolassee Town [95] about 7 miles from the Alibama Fort. They even promised to assist our People in doing it, and to stand by them if molested first by the French. For which they were to have a Quantity of ammunition for some Years, and Satisfaction for the Land. But that favourable Opportunity was neg-

Account of the Chicasaws there.

lected and lost.— The *Chicasaws* (about 80 Men) who live at their Camp on the Northern Frontier; near the head of the Coosaw River, prudently concern not themselves in the Creek Affairs. The chief Service they are of in that Post, is the guarding our Traders up and down in time of any Danger between their Nation and the Creek Country. As to the *Savanoes* [96] incor-

& Savanoes their Character.

porated or resident in the Creek Nation, altho' they are obliged

---

[93] The Upper Creeks lived on the Coosa and the Tallapoosa rivers. They were at times divided into the Abihka or Coosa branch and the Tallapoosa branch. Swanton, *Indian Tribes of North America*, p. 157. An Indian town called "Abeikas" on the upper Coosa appears in the Bowen map of 1763.

[94] Okfuskee town was located on the upper Tallapoosa River, occupied by the Okfuskee Creeks, an Upper Creek tribe.

[95] Muklasa town was located on the lower Tallapoosa River near the confluence with the Coosa. It was named after the Muklasa Creeks, an Upper Creek tribe.

[96] Or Shawnee. These Indians belonged to the Algonquian linguistic stock and were often called Savanoes or Savanoos. Their incredible wanderings have caused difficulty for investigators. Swanton, *Indian Tribes of North America*, pp. 227 ff.

Anecdotes con-
cerning them
&
their Disposition.

to observe the same Terms with us as that Nation doth, yet from their Character, and past Behaviour, their Disposition is much to be suspected. They are Stout, Bold, Cunning and the greatest Travellers in America. They lived heretofore on the River Savanoe, near Fort Moore; from whence on the breaking out of the Indian War in 1715 they fled Westerly with the Lower Creeks. Afterwards they withdrew to the Missisippi, and from thence it was not known for many Years where they were gone. In the beginning of 1744, some of them (45 Men) came to the Alibamaes, and settled in a Town by themselves about 7 miles below the Fort, and nearest to Mobile. Monsr. Vaudreüil, in his Letter to the Count de Maurepas at that time, called them *Chouanons,* and said they were theretofore Settled in Canada, where they were very well known to him. In the beginning of 1748, 140 Men more came to the [37] Coosaws, under a Leader named Peter Shartie, being a half breed by a Frenchman.[97] Having committed some Outrage or Violences in conjunction with some Frenchmen and a Party of their Indians from the Wabashe, on the back parts of Pensylvania & N. York; they embarked on the Aligany, and coming down the River Ohio, and up the great Cherokee River, landed N.N.E. from the Chicasaw Nation, and marched to the Creek Nation, where they were certainly expected by the French. For the Commander of the Alibama Fort had laid out Ground for them near that Garrison, and sent some Friends to meet and conduct them thither. But by the pressing Instances of our Traders, joined to the inclination of the Creeks, that [they] would Settle on the Northern Frontiers, 85 of them did settle in two Towns near the Chicasaw Camp. The rest incorporated (in all probability by the management of the French) in two of the Tallapoosee Towns, the most attached to us, Tuckabatchee & Muccolassee; the former being the Mother Town, and the latter that whereof the Chief (named the Wolf [98]) first offerd Land for us to build a Fort. Shartie

---

[97] Peter Chartier was the half-breed son of one Martin Chartier who accompanied La Salle's men and deserted in Illinois in 1680. Peter's mother was a Shawnee squaw. He was a licensed trader in Pennsylvania and later in the 1740's he was reported as a French agent. His band, known as Chartier's band, wandered from Mobile to the forks of the Ohio. See Pease, *Illinois on the Eve of the Seven Years' War,* pp. xxxix, 84-85, 185-86.

[98] The Wolf or Wolf King was a leading Upper Creek chief during the decade, 1755-1765. He appears to have been friendly with the English and in 1759 saved the lives of traders during a Creek uprising. Alden, *John Stuart,* p. 109.

sounded their name *Shawnoes or Shawanoes*. But the Creeks called them *Savanoes*; as did our Traders, who said they were the ancient Savanoes. The Cherokees also called them so; as they did likewise those with whom they had an Intercourse on the Ohio, commonly called Shawnoes in our Northern Colonies, and Chouanons by the French. There is a strong objection in the way; which is, that the Savanoes who fled from Savanoe River in So. Carolina in 1715, amounted only to 67 Men. On the other Hand, it is a fact, that a Catawba, who had been a Prisoner among the Shawnoes on the Ohio, and was sent home to his Nation in 1746 to invite two or three Head Men to go with others of the Cherokees, Creeks, and Chicasaws, to make a Peace together, brought that message as from the Savanoes, who said they only wanted to *return to their own Lands*. And it is as certain, that Shartie's Wife is an Apalatchee Woman. Now the Apalatchees who were brought away by Colonel Moore from their own Country, were settled by the Savanoes on Savano River; and some of them might when they fled together, have continued with them. I see no way of solving the Difficulty intirely, but by supposing, either that other Indians incorporated with the Savanoes at the Northward; or if the Shawnoes are a different People, that the Savanoes incorporated with them. But from hence there is room for the greater Apprehension, concerning the true Disposition of the Savanoes now in the upper Creek Nation. For they may [be] there ready to facilitate the opening a Communication that way with the Ohio & Illinois; or as some of them have discovered an Inclination to remove to the Cherokees, under a pretence of buying Goods Cheaper there, they may be made use of to help to open a Communication between Lake Erie and the Chattahuchee, through the Cherokee Nation, which hath already been too much Debauched, principally by means of the Savanoes or Shawanoes on the Ohio, who were employed as Emisaries and Agents by the French. And it is not at all improbable, that they may seek a Settlement near the mouth of that River, next to Apalatchee; which if they are devoted to the French, must be followed with the worst Consequence to us.

Chicasaws
their Situation

The Chicasaw Nation is situated further West, about Seven hundred and Eighty Miles from Charles Town; about 80 or 90 Miles to the Eastward of the Missippi, & less South of the great Cherokee River, at the head of the River Chactawhatchee; which taking its Rise from the same Ridge of Mountains as the Rivers in the upper Creek Country do, discharges itself also into the

Bay and harbour of Mobile. This therefore (with the Permission of the Chicasaws) may be another way of Communication from thence with the Ohio and Illinois. These Indians live in 7 Towns, having each a Pallisade Fort with a Ditch, in an open rich Champain Plaine about ten Miles in Circumference, [38] accessible only on one side, being almost surrounded by Swamps in a circular manner, about a Mile from any running Creek, and about 30 Miles from a place called the French Landing on the Chactawhatchee; which is as far as that River is Navigable with Boats. To the Westward a small River called the Chicasaw River, which takes its Rise about the midway from those Towns, inclining N.W. falls into the Missisippi. To the Northward, the Cherokee River joining the beforementioned United Streams of the Ohio, and Wabashe, flows together with them Westerly into the same— The Chicasaw Country is in itself a very fine one, being exceeding Fertile, Pleasant & Healthy. And in point of Situation without Doubt there is none other in the Western parts of No. America of so much Importance to the English to be possessed of. For it lies in a central place about the middle of the Missisippi, and commands all the water Passages between New Orleans and Canada, and from that River to the backs of our Colonies; And is Supportable, or accessible [by water] from most of them. There are in this Tract of Country, no less than three Important Places of Command over the Water Passages. At the mouth of the Hogohegee or great Cherokee River, the passage may be commanded not only up that River, but up the Wabashe and Ohio also. At their conflux or Junction with the Missisippi, the Passage not only of all those three Rivers, but of the Missisippi itself up and Down, between New Orleans and the Illinois, may be probably commanded also. Charlevoix who passed that way says, the Entrance of those Rivers (which he calls the Wabashe) into the Missisippi is scarce less than a Quarter of a League. I know not any one that hath given an Acct. of the breadth of the Missisippi itself at that conflux, nor have heard of any Englishman that ever saw it. Charlevoix remarks, "That in his Opinion there was not in all Louisiana a Place more proper for a Settlement than that; nor where it was of more Importance to have one. And that a Fort, with a good Garrison there, would curb the Indians, especially the Cherokees." Indeed it is not possible to cast an Eye ever so lightly over the Map, without being struck with the Importance of the Situation. If the French had a Settlement or Fort there on the

Importance of
the Possession
of that Country.

North Side, it would still be of no less Importance to us, to have one on the South, or Chicasaw side. And being so convenient, very distant Nations would find their way to it for Goods; which the French cannot render in those Parts, but at excessive rates, if at all— Again at the mouth of the Chicasaw River, the passage of the Missisippi may be commanded. Or if it is too wide in that part for firing a Shot across, it can scarce be doubted, that some Spot fit for that Purpose may be found between the aforesaid Conflux and the Chicasaw River, or the River Margot, where once was Fort Prudhomme; or even so low down as opposite to the Arkansas; All which Distance the Missisippi runs by the Chicasaw Country; and where a Shot may not be fired across the

their Character.

River, the defect may be supplied by armed Boats.— The Chicasaws are of all Indians the most Manly in their Persons, Sentiments, and Actions; being of large gracefull figure, open Countenance and Manners, and generous Principles; Vigorous, Active, Intrepid, and Sharp in appearance even to Feirceness; expert Horsemen (having perhaps the finest breed of Horses in No. America); by much the best Hunters; and without Exception (by the acknowledgment of all Europeans [39] as well as Indians that know them, who respect them as such) the best

Anecdotes
concerning them,
& the French.

Warriours. Even their Women handle Arms, and face an Enemy like Men. They first put a stop formerly to the Spanish Conquests under Ferdinand de Soto. They are the only Indians that ever came voluntarily to a general Engagement with Europeans in open Ground; as they did with the French in 1736; when after repelling an Attack made upon one of their Towns by some chosen old regular Troops, under excellent Officers, Superior in Number, and assisted by three times as many Indians, they engaged them in an open Plain; and having totally defeated them, pursued them with great Slaughter a considerable Distance. In a Subsequent & more formidable Invasion in 1739 by three times their number of [French] Troops, and as many Indians also, the Chicasaws went to meet them; and having obliged them to entrench themselves they even ventured (a thing before unheard of) to attack them in their Trenches which they entered [&] after making great Havock, put the rest all to Flight. In 1742 they defeated intirely a double Invasion made at the same time from different Quarters, to wit, by 2000 Chactaws, headed by only 10 French Men from N. Orleans or Mobile, and 500 Troops besides Indians from Canada, of which last, few ever returned. And in 1753 the last year they repelled another attempt made upon them. All those Invasions were undertaken by the French, professedly in order to extirpate the Chicasaw Nation. Yet such is the magnanimity of those Indians, that under those Circumstances they never asked the Assistance of any of their Neighbours; being aided only by the Presents of ammunition which they have received occasionally from the South Carolina Government; and being advised, in regard to their future Safety, to remove and live nearer to their Friends, they resolved never to leave their Country, declaring in their way of Expression, that they would go again into the same Ground they came out of. But for their better Defence and Security against any Surprize, they built a Pallisade Fort in each of their Towns and made a Ditch round it; And did ask for some Swivel Guns from us, tho' indeed they did not obtain them. The Inveteracy of the French towards this Nation is intirely owing to their Heady Attachment to the English, the Weight they bear among all the Nations, round them, and for that [the] free Navigation of the Missisippi, and Communication between New Orleans and Montreal, or the Illinois, depends almost intirely upon them. They Traded with the English before the French enter'd the Missisippi; whom they never liked, and therefore would have no Freindship with them. As the French endeavoured arbitrarily to put a stop to the Commerce, which the Nations upon and near that River had with us after, in like manner as before they came to those parts, the Chicasaws formed a plan for their Expulsion; and Sheltered and Protected the remains of the Unhappy Natchees, who were almost totally extinguished in a Premature Attempt to assert their Natural Rights.[99] By which means the Chicasaws drew on themselves the first Resentment of the French. And in order to distress them, the French have done their utmost in times of Peace with us, to intimidate and stop the English Traders from continuing their Trade with that Nation, by causing some of them to be assasinated on the Path to it, and their Horses to be Stolen and Driven off from their Range near the Towns, to Tambekbe Fort; to which place four of the Traders (by name Godfrey Harding, Florence Agan, Clarke & Picket) being decoyed, under Pretence of redelivering their Horses, were made Prisoners and carried to Mobile, where they Suffered Severe Treatment in Jail for 2 or 3 Years (as it

---

[99] Adair confirms the part played by the Chickasaw in the uprising. *Adair's History*, p. 379.

were interrorem),[100] upon an Allegation that they had assisted the Chicasaws in Fight when Invaded; and were then sent to Brest, from whence [40] Picket made his Escape, Clark was induced by hardships to turn Catholick and marry there, and the other two were seen in Prison in 1747 by some of our People, who were then put into the same as prisoners of War; and tis thought those two are there still. The French having undertaken so many Expeditions tho' unsuccessfull against the Chicasaws, & set all the Indians upon them on whom they had any Influence, the Chicasaws, on the Arrival of Monsr. Vaudreuil as new Governour of Louisiana in 1743, Sending him a Present of some French Prisoners they had just taken at the Arkansas, signified their desire to forbear Hostilities and live in Peace. But that Govr. refused to be at Peace with them, but on *Condition they would drive the English out of their Country;* which they having declined to do, and he having prevailed in particular on the numerous Chactaws not to make Peace with them, he wrote to the Govr. of Canada (which Letter was intercepted) "That in order to oblige the Chicasaws to perform his will, he would cause them to be harder pushed than ever by War; and pressed him to engage the Northern Nations also to fall upon them with more Vigour than ever." Accordingly they have been since press'd on all sides by the united measures of those two Governours. So that after the same manner, in which they have for many Years past been gradually Diminished little by little, they must in process of time be totally extirpated, unless timely Supported by some other means than have hitherto been used. The severe measures of the French, have rivetted in them an implacable Enmity towards them, and attached them the more firmly to us, as their only Dependance. Their Policy hath been ever uniformly, to Cultivate a Friendship with all the Indian Nations in Alliance with the English; And they have done their utmost endeavour to incite other Nations to War with the French. For which purpose they sent their Calumet many Years ago so far as the Miamis or Twightwees, at the head of the Wabashe at the West End of Lake Erie, on the road to Canada; and in 1746, Twenty of them went so far as the Sennikas, and made a proposal to joyn them in making War upon Canada. In a word: there is nothing we can propose to them with regard to the French, but what we may assure ourselves they will most gladly come into; And it will be our own Fault therefore, if we do

*their Policy
&
Disposition.*

---

[100] As a warning in order to terrify or deter others.

not make a valuable use of their Friendship & Disposition. For I doubt not they would for a proper Support or Protection, surrender their whole Country to his Majesty.

The Chactaw Nation, is situated lower down on the West Side of the same River Chactawhatchee, at the distance of Seven hundred & Thirty Miles from Charles Town; the nearest Towns to the Chicasaws, being about one hundred & Twenty Miles to the Southward thereof. The Importance of their Situation consists wholly in their being a Frontier to the French Settlements round N. Orleans and Mobile, which therefore they may either Protect or ravage. For which reason it is most the Interest of the French, to manage that Nation. They have a Fort there named Tombekbe on the side of the River at the entrance of the direct Path from the upper Creeks into the Nation. To avoid which our Traders go round by way of the Chicasaws; which makes their Journey about Two Hundred Miles the more.— Of all the Indians the Chactaws bear the worst Character. They are

Subtle, Decietfull, Insolent, Lucrative, Beggarly, Vicious, and Indolent to such a degree, that for want of Planting Corn sufficient, living for the most part miserably, they eat Creatures and things untasted by other Indians. And withal they are less Warlike than those before Described; insomuch that Govr. Vaudreüil, in a Letter to the French Secretary of State, said, "That he believed the Chicasaws, if they had to do with them only (tho' near 10 times their Number) would in the end Destroy them." [41] The Chactaws are indebted to the French themselves perhaps, for some part of their sd. Character.[101] In Craft and Breach of Promises they have but too well imitated them. Their Insolence arises from their knowledge of the Importance their Friendship is of from their Vicinity to the French, and the Court paid to them on that account. They are lucrative, because the French Commerce, not being sufficiently valuable, it hath put them [upon] a way of, in a manner selling the French just as much Friendship as they pay for. Their beggarly Quality is the result of their Poverty, and the Habit they have accquired in making the most out of the French; in like manner as their carnal Vice is the result of their lazy Life.— They are seldom

---

101 Atkin's dislike for the French is reflected in his contempt for the Choctaw. In his Choctaw revolt memoir, he emphasizes the better qualities of these Indians. Adair also speaks of them critically, mentioning their "fickle, treacherous, and bloody a disposition." *Adair's History*, p. 305.

Anecdotes
concerning them
with regard to
the English &
the French.

engaged in War with any of our Friends (indeed they are mostly too remote), but with the Chicasaws occasionally, and against their Inclination, by the Instigation of, and generally in Conjunction with the French. As they had a Trade with the English before the French came to those parts, a Comparison between the Quality of each of their Goods, and the full supply of those of the former & the scantiness of those of the latter, hath often inclined them to endeavour to regain the Trade with us. Govr. Vaudreüil, in a Letter which he wrote jointly with the Comissary of the Marine, to the French Secretary of State, after his first general meeting with the Indians at Mobile, upon his coming to the Government of Louisiana complained, "of the Inability they the French had constantly laid under to supply all the Goods necessary for their Consumption. That they had often promised to Furnish them, but had not been able to do it. And that most of the Indians in their Speeches insinuated, that they had not kept their word." However the Trade with us by the direct way through the upper Creek Nation, is effectually curbed and restrained by the Albama and Tombekbe Forts. And as oft as it hath been, by the encouragement of any of the Chactaw Towns, introduced by way of the Chicasaws; the French have found means to interrupt and put a Stop to it, by hiring their partizans to kill some of our Traders on the Path. This was more particularly the case some time after the Chactaw great Chief or King (commonly called Red Shooes) had been with many of his Head Men down to Charles Town in 1738, and made the first solemn Treaty of Peace and Commerce with the Government of So. Carolina. In 1746 indeed, the French during the War with us, not being able to supply Goods to the Chactaws who were almost Naked, Red Shooes, with the almost general Consent of the Nation, came to an open Rupture with them by Blows; and sent his Brother to Charles Town to make Satisfaction for what had passed; who in the beginning of 1747 [102] made a Second Treaty, offering to put their Fidelity to the Proof by attacking and taking Tombekbe Fort by Surprise; and by assisting also to take the Alibama Fort. But being at first Neglected, and afterwards not duly supported, when in Confidence of being supplied with ammunition they had pushed the French to such Extremities that they were actually quitting Tombekbe Fort, and

[102] Confirmed in Alden, *John Stuart*, p. 28. Also see Atkin's "The Choctaw Revolt" for an elaboration of the Choctaw rebellion.

the Inhabitants in the Country round Mobile were driven from their Settlements into the Town, but the French taking the advantage of the Distress to which the Chactaws themselves were at length reduced for want of Ammunition, fell on them with the few remains of their Party and made great Slaughter repeatedly; the Chactaws having in vain implored Succour, and not to be left to fall a Sacrifice to the French, finding themselves still unsupported, and oppressed with the miseries of a Civil War, their King and his Brother, extinct, some of both parties went together to Mobile the latter End of 1749, and made their Peace with the French, being in a manner compelled thereto. In consequence thereof our Traders were soon scalped again as before by Virtue of Publick Rewards; and in 1751 not any venturing into the Nation, an intire stop was put to the Trade. In the Year following even one that was employed to carry Presents to the Nations, having one of his Men killed on the Path, returned without [42] delivering them. Undoubtedly we have still a small party in that Nation for us. And such is the Boldness or Rashness of our Traders, that upon the least Encouragement or hopes of Success, some or other of them will without a Licence run the hazard of going wth. Goods. But surely that ought not to be tol[l]erated. For besides that the Crown thereby often looses the Lives of Subjects, together with their Substance; if while any Nation of Indians commit Hostile Acts upon any of our People, they can still have our Goods for which alone they value our Friendship, we cannot reasonably expect to make them our Friends. And therefore in good Policy, we ought to oblige them to court us for our Goods, and Friendship, with their own. When the Civil War begun among the Chactaws, the upper Creeks advised them to deal as they did in a Friendly manner with both the English and the French. And the French at that time would have been glad of it. But the two parties could not then agree upon that Measure. And when the Brother of Red Shoes was in Charles Town making a Second Treaty, an objection being made to the Sending Traders to their Nation, in regard to their Personal Safety, seeing Tambekbe Fort stood in their way, he proposed to move their Towns nearer towards the English. Of that Disposition a very good use might be made. For as there are two intermediate Rivers between the Coosaw & Chactawhatchee or the upper Creek Nation, and the Chactaw Nation, to wit, the Cohahawbahatchee &

Computation
of Miles in
this Acco.

the Pattagahatchee,[103] at present both unpossessed, if a Block-house were built on one of those Rivers, to which such of the Chactaws as were in our Interest might withdraw, our Traders might trade with them in all Security, and save three hundred Miles [travelling] up and the like down again.

It may be proper to be noticed, That the Miles hereinbefore mentioned on several Occasions, are not Geometrical, but travelling Miles on the Road. And that the Horse Carriage of Goods to each Indian Nation respectively, except the Catawbas, is 150 Miles less from the Embarkadeer at Fort Moore, or Augusta on Savano River, than it is from Charles Town; or 275 Miles less to the Creeks, Chicasaws, and Chactaws, from Echeteo on a Branch of the Alatamha River, where there might be the like Embarkadeer.

Having given an Account of the Situation, Character, and Disposition of the several Indian Nations, that have any Inter-course or Connection with South Carolina; I proceed now humbly to propose the following Plan [43]

---

[103] Atkin apparently refers to the Cahaba and Black Warrior rivers. See the John Mitchell map of 1755.

Echeteo, mentioned below, is called Echetee O[ld] T[own] on the Mitchell map and was apparently located near the headwaters of the Ocmulgee River in what is now north central Georgia. This town was undoubtedly named after the "Echito" Indians of the Lower Creeks who were of the Hitchiti group and "spoke related languages distinct from the Muskogee." Swanton, *Early History of the Creek Indians and Their Neighbors,* pp. 172, 405. The map in *Adair's History* (frontispiece) locates "Echete" on the upper Oconee River. This later map differs to a con-siderable degree from the John Mitchell map on the location of Indian towns.

THE PLAN FOR

IMPERIAL INDIAN CONTROL

*Plan of a general Direction & Management of the
Indian Affairs throughout North America, under one
uniform Regulation of their Commerce, for retriev-
ing & establishing the British Interest among the
Indian Nations, & thereby the future Security of our
Colonies against the Designs of the French*

Vizt.

That his Majesty be graciously pleased to take under his immediate Direction whatever concerns the Affairs of the Indian
Nations & their Commerce, by Parlimentary Authority; to be
executed under his Royal Commission & Instructions conformable
thereto, in the manner hereafter mentioned. And that all Acts
or Clauses of Acts now in Force in the several Colonies that
have any relation to the Indians or their Trade, and are not
compatable with or subservient to this Plan, be repealed or made
null according to the Opinion of the Right Honble. the Lords
Commissioners for Trade & Plantations.

That all the Indian Nations or Tribes be divided into two
Districts; the Northern District from Nova Scotia to Virginia
inclusive, comprehending the Six United Nations of N. York
with their immediate Dependants chiefly on the Waters of the
Ohio, & those commonly called the Eastern Indians, or any
others to the Westward; And the southern District of North
Carolina, South Carolina, & Georgia, comprehending the Cherokees, and all the other Nations, particularly the Catawbas, Chicasaws, Creeks, & Chactaws, living independent of each other, to
the South of the Hogohegee or great Cherokee River, (which
is a kind of natural Boundary from East to West between the
two Districts) and to the westward thereof so far back at least
as the Missisippi.

That two fit Persons, who are already personally accquainted
with the Indians and their Affairs, be appointed by his Majesty,
with proper Salaries, to go properly attended, and provided with
Presents, in quality of Envoys to the Indian Nations, one to each
District; who may propose, and make a new Treaty with them
Severally in his Majesty's Name. The principal Articles whereof
on the part of the Indians to be

1st That they shall not permit any other Europeans but the
English, to deal or traffick with them, or build Forts, or even
Houses among them.

Plan of a General
Direction & Man-
agement of the
Indian Affairs
throughout
No. America.

2d That they shall not admit any English Traders to traffick among them, without producing a Licence for it by the Kings Authority, as after mentioned.

3. That they shall not come into any of the English Plantations or actual Settlements, in order to Hunt, Traffick, or for any other purpose whatever, without previous Notice and Leave obtained from the Governour of the Province.

4. That they shall do their utmost to prevent, or to give Satisfaction proportioned to the Offence, for any Violence or Injury offer'd to any Englishman in his Person or Effects.

5. That they shall treat all our Friends as their Friends, and our Enemies as their Enemies, and assist us accordingly on all occasions. And

6. That they shall not sell Lands to any of the Kings Subjects, but to his Majesty only. In consideration of which, the Condition on his Majestys part in the said Treaty to be

[44] 1st That a Fort, or strong Blockhouse picquetted, Shall be built in each Nation that desire it, (not having one already) as well for their Protection against their Enemies, as for the Security of our Traders and their Effects; such Nations setting apart, and giving the most proper Spot of Ground for the Purpose, and a sufficient Quantity of Land adjoining for the use of the Garrisons. And also assisting our People with Labour in buildg the Forts, and with Provisions the first year.

2. That their Guns and Hatchets shall be mended there Gratis.

3. That they shall be supplied with all kinds of Goods for their use, the prices being fixed at the most moderate Terms between them and our Traders; And that they shall be visited annually by the Persons hereafter named, who shall enquire into the Behaviour of the Traders, hear Complaints and Punish them for any Frauds or abuses committed; And who shall at the same time Consult with their Chiefs, severally in each Nation, as well as at any other time with the Chiefs of the several Nations that shall be in Friendship with us, and with each other, at certain places of general meeting, upon whatever concerns their and our Welfare; in order to perpetuate a Friendship between them and us.

That the said Envoys be also constituted Commissioners General (or by some other Title) on his Majestys behalf; one to each District, independent of any particular Governor, or Provincial Authority, for regulating the Commerce in manner hereafter mentioned; for inspecting the Behaviour of the Traders in the several Nations; consulting with the Indian Chiefs; and negotiating whatever Affairs, concern the Indians for the future. And in order that they may have full Weight, as well in the Eyes of the Indians as of the Traders, and be enabled to maintain their Authority, and effectually promote the Service.

That they be vested likewise with the chief Command of all Forts & Garrisons built or to be built in the Indian Countries; and so as not to interfere with any military Command given by his Majesty to a General Officer.— And in order to put a due check upon the Power & Authority of the said Officers, as well in behalf of the Crown, as for the Satisfaction and Security of the People of our several Colonies, who will be greatly interested in their Conduct and Behaviour, and who 'tis proposed by this Plan shall in some Shape or other defray the chief part of the Expence thereof;

That one fit person, having some knowledge or accquaintance with Indian Affairs, be deputed by the Governour & Council of each Province to accompany & assist the said Commissioners General, at the annual Visitations of each Nation, or at the General Meetings of the Indian Chiefs in their respective Districts; who may represent the several Provinces or Colonies to the Indians, and also serve in the nature of a Council to the Commissioners, and by whose advice all Talks shall be given by them to the Indians, subsequent Treaties made, Presents Distributed, the Rates of Goods ascertained, Licences to Traders of each Province indifferently granted, Instructions given therewith, Determinations made upon the Offences of the Traders, and all Expences in General incurred, and measures taken, other than shall be expressly warranted by his Majesty. The said Deputies to have a proper Allowance for that Service out of a Provincial Fund to be established as aftermentioned.

That neither the said Commissioners, or Provincial Deputies, nor any other [45] Officer or Person to be employed in the Publick Service, in the Indian Countries, be concerned in the Trade directly or indirectly, under a Severe Penalty.

That one of his Majesty's Sub Engineers, be sent with each Commissioner, who may make Choice of the Ground for the Forts and Blockhouses to be built at his Majesty's Charge, in their respective Districts, prepare the plans thereof to be approved of by the Commissioners, and likewise see the Work executed according to Contracts or Estimates of the Expence, to be approved by the said Commissioners and Provincial Deputies—

That the number of Companies of Foot Soldiers in his Majestys Service at present independent in the Provinces of N. York and So. Carolina, be augmented and incorporated into two Compleat Regiments, one for the particular Service of each District, chiefly to do Garrison Duty. By which means there being always Field Officers on the Spot, the Militia of the different Provinces will upon occasion more chearfully joyn and obey their Command; whereas Captains of Companies are not esteemed of that Consequence. For the encouragement of Men to inlist as Recruits in those Regiments, that they may have leave to be discharged at a certain time, giving three Months [Notice] of their Intention; by which means military Dicipline will be propagated among the People of the Colonies.

That the several Forts and Blockhouses be garrisoned, by Detachments from the said Regiments. The same to be releived, one half only at a time annually; To the Intent that the Men in Garrison, and the Indians, may not be at any time intirely Strangers to each others Persons & manners; but that their Knowledge and Accquaintance therewith may be introduced, preserv'd, and transferrd imperceptibly; And so as that none of the Officers or Men may remain longer than two Years in the same Garrison; Provided that such Men may be permitted to do it as shall take Indian Wives; by which means our Interest among the Indians will be strengthened both by the Women, and their Breed proving the hardiest and best attached. And therefore it will be prudent to encourage such Marriages.— And for the Encouragement of the said Garrisons.

1st. That 2d. pr. Diem each Man additional Pay from the Provincial Fund, be given to them, to enable them to purchase Corn & other Necessaries from the Indians, or to raise the same themselves.

2. That Ground be allotted each Man, for planting Corn, Tobacco, or other Necessaries.

3. That they be allowed the same pr. Diem, for their Labour in helping to build or repair Forts, as is Customary in the Army.

4. That they be permitted to go out by Turns, not exceeding 3 or 4 at once, with or without Indians, to Hunt for their own Account; by which means they will become good Woodsmen, and fit for Expeditions.

5. That for the particular Encouragement of the Officers, as well as in part of the Men, seeing Money, for want of Currency, is of no Value in the Indian Countries, and our Traders demand great Prices there for Goods; therefore the said Officers be allowed to pay the Men their pay (that is such of them as shall be willing so to receive it) in Necessaries for their use, rated moderately between them previously by the Commissioners and Provincial Deputies; so that the Men may be supplied with the same Cheaper than from the Traders, and at the same time the Officers may have some Recompence for their Trouble and Risque in making such Provision for them.

That in each Fort or Blockhouse, that is in each Nation, there be fixed a Gunsmith inlisted, and to receive besides his Soldiers Pay an extra adequate Allowance out of the Provincial Fund; who shall be obliged, without any Reward whatever from the Indians, to repair & mend their Guns, & Grind their Hatchets. The same Men to act as Armourers and Gunners of the Forts.

That a Sworn Interpreter be employed to reside at or near each Fort, who at first for [46] sometime may be one of the Traders of fairest Character, and who without any or but little Expence may be satisfied for his Trouble in manner herein after mentioned— And that two Sharp Solid Lads, inlisted, or as Covenant Servants to the Commissioners for the time being, be placed also in each Fort, in order to qualify them to succeed the said Interpreters as such; the better to attain which, they should pass part of their time with some of the Indians at their Houses in the Neighbourhood; the Indians having often lamented the want of good Interpreters, as well as of honest and Disinterested ones; the Traders interpreting so much and in such manner as they think fit for their Purpose. The rest of their Time those Lads might be assistant to the Gunsmiths, and Qualify themselves to serve as such.

That a Missionary be sent (not very Young) to each Fort, with a proper Salary, by the Society for Propagating the Gospel in forriegn Parts;[104] who by performing the Offices of the Church, may influence the Lives and Morals of the Soldiers & Traders, and create respect for us among the Indians.

That those Missionaries be also for their Encouragement appointed Commissaries and Storekeepers, with an additional Salary out of the Provincial Fund, to take Charge of the King's Stores, and of the Presents for Indians; and to keep account of the

---

104 Chartered in 1701 and actively promoted by Thomas Bray, Anglican clergyman who served as commissary in Maryland.

Expending and Distribution thereof. They may also be empowered, in conjunction with the Commanding Officers of the Forts, to bestow Presents of small Value upon the old Leading Indians, occasionally between the general Visitations of the Commissioners. Their Accounts to be audited at those times by the Commissioners and Deputies.

That there be two Troops of Rangers, composed of Men used to the Woods, to be paid out of the Provincial Fund; one to attend each Commissioner, with the Provincial Deputies of his District, when they go to make the first Treaty with the Indian Nations, & at all Visitations afterwards, as well for the Safety of their Persons, as to support the Dignity of his Majesty Commission. Two of which Rangers to be Quarter'd at all other times at each Fort, in order to carry Expresses. And the rest to be employed in Ranging on the back of the Settlements of the several Provinces, in such manner as shall be found most Convenient for their Protection. For which purpose they should carry some Dogs with them, the more effectually to Discover Sculking Indians by their Scent. Whereby the Indians will be terrified, and the back Settlers rendered Quiet and Safe in their Plantations. Those Rangers not to be Compellable to serve longer than from Year to Year; but any of them to be discharged at the years end, giving three months Notice of their Intention.

That a Secretary be allowed to each Commissioner for the Service of each District, who shall in particular keep a Journal of all Proceedings; a Copy whereof to be transmitted annually to the Right Honble. the Lords Commissioners for Trade & Plantations, in the same manner as the Journals of the Council are transmitted by the Governours of the Several Provinces. By which means the Indian Affairs, which have hitherto lain too much in the Dark, will become well known & understood in England; and the true State of them at any time seen at one View. The said Journals to be open at all times to the Inspection of the Governours & Councils; by which means, together with the Personal Knowledge of their Deputies, they may preserve their Accquaintance with the Indian Affairs, & be enabled to make [47] any observations upon the proceedings of the Commissioners, for the Service of the Crown, or of any particular Colony.

That the Commissioners and Provincial Deputies, do visit all the Nations, and Forts or Blockhouses in their Turn, Yearly; except the most Distant, such as the Chicasaws about 800 Miles (and the Chactaws when in Friendship with us); whom it may be Sufficient perhaps to visit every other Year. Those annual Visitations to be made at such time as shall not interfere with the planting Season of the Indians in the Spring; or with their Hunting Season in the Winter.

That some certain Allowance be made to the Commissioners, for the Expences of their Journies, and for entertaining the Indians at all Visitations or Meetings; as well as for Occasional Interpreters. And some certain Allowance also to the Commanding Officers of the Forts, for Liquor which they must give to some of the Head Men, who will visit them from time to time.

That Presents, besides those to be delivered from the King at making the new Treaty, be annually distributed by the Commissioners among the Indian Chiefs of each Nation at the Visitations, purchased out of the Provincial Fund. In doing which great regard should be had to their respective importance. And that some Presents of small Value be left at the same time with the Commissaries at the Forts, to be given Occasionally the Year round between the Visitations, in conjunction with the Commanding Officers, to the old Leading Men.

That as those Presents are to be given as a token of his Majestys Friendship for the Indians, so care should be taken to let them know, That the like Token is expected on their Part in Exchange, tho' inferiour in Value according to their Poverty. And they might be brought to offer one Deer Skin each Gunman annually, if he were to receive a greater Quantity of Ammunition to his Share than he could have for it from a Trader. By which means as the Skins might be still worth more than the Cost of the Ammunition, the Presents might be made on both sides on very good Terms; especially if the Traders were to carry the Kings Presents, as they should, free of Charge; And the number of Fighting Men would be also thereby annually known. Besides by this method of giving Presents to the Indians in their own Country, they will not only be more valuable to them, but the great Expences, and all the Inconveniences attending their Visits in our Settlements, would be saved to the Several Colonies.

That the Commanding Officers and Commissaries at the several Forts, do jointly correspond with the Commissioner General in their respective District, upon all Occurrences that may happen between the Visitations; and take their Directions thereupon, excepting in such matters as shall be left to their Discretion.

That the Commissioners do correspond, and cooperate from time to time as Occasion may offer, with each other, and with the several Governours, for the general Service; And also Correspond with the Lords for Trade, to keep their Lordships accquainted with all Events.

That they do make use of a well known Seal of Office, having some fit Device adapted to the Ideas of the Indians, and distinguished from each other.

That in case of their Death, the Provincial Deputy of N. York be allowed to Succeed and Officiate in the room of the Commissioner General for the Northern District, until his Majestys pleasure shall be known; and the Provincial Deputy of South Carolina [48] in the like manner in the room of the Commissioner General for the Southern District. Which will be some further inducement for the fittest Persons, in those Provinces which are the most Interested in, and accquainted with the Indian Affairs, to serve as Deputies.

That the places of General Meeting at any time between the King's Commissioners and the Provincial Deputies, and the Indian Chiefs of each Nation in alliance with us and with each other, be, to wit; in the Northern District, at Onondaga, where the Six United Nations hold their General Councils (and not at Albany, where the Indians are not by this Plan to be permitted even to trade for the future); and in the Southern District, at the Fort to be built in the Lower Cherokee Nation, being the most convenient & proper Place in the present Situation of Affairs, with respect to the white People or Indians, as it is the most central in particular to the upper Cherokee Nation (across whose whole Country it is near 150 Miles), to the upper and lower Creek Nations, the Lower Chicasaws, and the Catawbas. And it is the more proper that the meetings should be in the Cherokee Country, because that Nation hath made a Treaty already with his Majesty, by Deputies sent to England for that purpose in 1730, and repeatedly since pressed us to build Forts in their Country, which is a good Example for other Nations. The said Fort to be built at or near Toogoloo,[105] the principal Town, or such other Frontier Town as shall be found fittest to serve as a Barrier, between the Cherokees and our Settlements in So. Carolina and Georgia, most equally alike; and also be-

---

[105] Tugaloo was a former Cherokee town on the river of the same name in Habersham County, Georgia.

tween them and the Lower Creeks (That erected sometime since near Keowee is neither so Situated, nor in itself tis apprehended, of much Value or Consequence). Which Fort in the Lower Cherokee Nation is as necessary, for being a Curb upon the Behaviour of the Cherokees themselves, and upon the Northern French Indians going that way into our Settlements, and against the Catawbas, and also upon the Young Cherokees interrupting the Peace that may be made with the Creeks; as a Fort is necessary in the upper Cherokee Nation also, for their Protection against the Northern Indians in the French Interest, and to keep out the French from taking footing there.

That the Indian Trade or Commerce be Regulated after the following manner, Vizt.

1st. After the said Commissioners shall have gone to the Indian Nations, made known his Majesty's kind Intentions in sending them, and made a Treaty with them on the terms before mentioned, that then they do immediately each in his District, with the advice of the Provincial Deputies, agree upon and ascertain the Valuation of all Goods to be carried for the use of the Indians, and of Deer Skins Leather & Furs in barter for the same, at moderate equitable, and fair Rates, between the Traders and the Indians; due regard being had to the respective Cost and Value in the places of Import & Export, & to the Charge, risque, and trouble of conducting the Trade. Those Rates to be confirmed, or alterd, every succeeding Year, as may appear reasonable. And the Indians should engage to render the Deer Skins clean trimmed, free from Snouts and Shanks, in regard to their Preservation from Worm, and cheaper Carriage— As the Hazards attending the Indian Trade, which have been the chief Cause of the great prices exacted of the Indians for Goods by the Traders, will be far less as soon as the Proposed Forts are Built, tis presumed those Prices may be much reduced; which will ingratiate us very much with the Indians.

2. That together with a Commission in the Kings Name in the usual Manner, (accompanied with a Scarlet or Red Coat & Breeches, Gun, Cutlass &c) to each Chief or Head Man of a Nation, [49] or Tribe, or (where there are a great many Towns, as among the Cherokees and Creeks) of a Town or Towns containing not less than a certain Number of Gunmen, the said Commissioners do deliver a Pair of small Scales and Weights, sufficient to weigh 3. 2. 1. and ½ Pound; and also a Yard made

of Copper, standard Weight and Measure; by which the Goods of every Trader respectively allowed to Trade with such Nation, Tribe, Town or Towns, and the Skins and Furrs sold to him, shall be Weighed and Measured. Whereby all Frauds in that way will for the future be prevented, to the great Content of the Indians. The said Head Men to attend at the annual Meetings, to represent their Towns, and give account of the Behaviour of the Traders— The second Head Man to every such Head Man (who may have a Blue Cloth Coat faced with Red & Breeches &c), in case of his Death or Absence to stand in his Stead. It is most eligible to have the Trade of every Nation carried on at the Fort therein. But that method would probably create Discontent with the Cherokees & Creeks, who have been always used to have the Convenience of a Trader in most of their Towns. Yet it might be attempted, making use of great Caution. The Traders would be kept still better in order, and more Secure; and they would be a Support, and of Service to the Forts.

3. That as no Person is to be admitted by the Indians to Trade with them, without producing a licence by the King's Authority from one of the Commissioners General; every Person applying to either of them for such Licence, shall bring a Certificate from some Magistrate or Clergman in the Parish or County of his Residence, or from the Provincial Deputy of the Province, testifying under his hand and Seal, "That having Published his Intention at least ten Days at the Church Door or in some other publick manner, no reasonable Objection hath been made to him, but that he appears to be of honest Repute and Sober Life & Conversation." Out of which Persons, the Commissioners (each in his District) shall with the advice of the Provincial Deputies, make Choice of such and so many to be Traders with the Indians as shall be thought proper; and shall grant Licences accordingly to them for that purpose under his hand & Seal of Office, to be in force not exceeding one Year, expressing therein respectively, the Nation, Town, or Towns wherein such Traders are to reside, and not to transgress the same; Every such Trader entering into a Penal Bond with Surety to his Majesty, "That he and the Men employed under him, (whose names being of Honest repute and Sober Life also, shall be inserted in his Licence) will Demean themselves well towards the Indians; and that he will observe and Obey the Instructions to be given pursuant to the Regulations established by the advice also of the Provincial Deputies, and annexed to his Licence, as well as all other lawfull

Orders and Instructions that may be given from time to time."
Which Licence shall be produced and shown by every such
Trader immediately on his Arrival in the Nation, or Town men-
tioned in the same, to the Commissioned Head Man of the
Place, before he may presume to Trade there. The said Head
Men to be at Liberty to seize for their use the Effects of any
Persons that shall go to Trade with them without having such
Licence. By which means all irregular, Vagrant, and disorderly
Traders, living fixed under no particular Government, or ram-
bling at large among Indians within the limits of another
Governt., and therefore hitherto not made accountable to any
for their Actions, will be totally Suppressed; as well to the great
Satisfaction of the Indians themselves, as to the Peace & Security
of the Colonies—

4. That no Tax, Duty, or Impost whatever shall be paid by the
Traders, for or on Account of the Goods carried to or brought
from any of the Indian Nations. Which, together with the Re-
duction of the present Rates exacted by the Traders, will render
it impossible for the French to Rival us with the Indians in
the Cheapness of Goods.

5. That every Trader be laid particularly under the following
Obligations, to wit.

[50] 1st. To carry among his Cargoes of Goods, a sufficient
Quantity of good Powder & Ball, proportioned to the number
of Indians he is to Trade with. That so they may not be obliged
to have recourse to the French, as they have been for that
necessary Article, which is their only means for purchasing
Every thing else.

2. Not to carry more Rum or other Spirits with them, than a
certain limited Quantity for their own private use, and to give
their Friends among the Indians now and then a Dram. But to
incur a penalty for any Indian getting Drunk with such
Liquo[u]r, that being the only Cause of almost every mischief
they do; & the greatest Destruction of their Numbers.

3. Not to Credit any one Indian for more than one pound
Weight of powder & four pounds of Bullets; being sufficient to
fit him out either for War or Hunting. Which will prevent for
the future, the many evil Consequences arising hitherto from
the Indians being in Debt to our Traders; especially if the
Indians are discharged from paying any greater Debts.

4. Not to Defraud, Injure, or Abuse the Indians by any means whatsoever; but to be kind to them, and Conform strictly to the Rates, Weights, and Measures established for Goods. Whereby the affections of the Indians, many of whom have been alienated by Abuses, may be best regain'd.

5. Not to Trade with any Subjects of the Crown of France in the Indian Country, more especially in Forts, under a severe Penalty. Nor with Indians of any Nation not living in Alliance or Friendship with his Majestys Subjects; unless they come for Goods. By which means our Friendship will be courted.

6. Not to presume to talk with the Indians upon, or intermeddle with matters of State & Government.

7. To carry when required to the Indian Country free of Expence, his Quota of the Presents to be given annually; in proportion to the number of Boats, Horses, or Carriages, employed by him in the Trade.

8. To appear Personally at the Visitation or meeting of the Commissioner General & Provincial Deputies, with the Indian Chiefs, in order to answer any Complaint; and at the same time to surrender his Licence and Instructions, that no further use may be made thereof with the Indians after new Licences shall be granted. One of his Men may be left to [take] care of his Effects (but not to Trade) during his Absence on that Occasion, or while he goes once in the Year only, to transact the concerns of his Trade in the Province to which [he] belongs.

6. That, in regard to the great Difficulty of weaning the Indians intirely from Rum or other Spirits, to which they have been too much accustomed, and which cannot therefore be attempted at once without producing perhaps too great a Discontent, but must be done gradually; one Trader (and no more) may be Licenced to sell Rum or other Spirits in each Nation—Which Person to be (by way of Recompence) the Trader who is to be employed as Interpreter, residing at or near the Fort, so as to be under the Inspection of the Commanding Officer, or Commissary. The Rum or Spirits on its arrival, to be Lodged in the Fort under Lock, and to be temper'd in their Presence with a certain proportion of Water, before any of it be delivered out again for the Indians. None to be delivered on any pretence to any but a Commissioned Chief, or a Messenger from him bringing a Token to be agreed on for the purpose, at well known fix'd Periods only, such as at every New or Full Moon; And to

whom may be then sold a certain limited Quantity, for each Man belonging to the Town or Towns of such Chief.

7. That, in order to render Drunkenness shamefull in the Eyes of the Indians, by the Example of our own People, and thereby to produce as much as possible that Regularity and Decency [51] of manners between them, which is necessary to the Security of our Colonies, the private Soldiers and Servants of the Traders who may at any time get Drunk, shall be exposed to view in some ludicrous manner or other. And the Trader himself shall, for the first Offence incur a Penalty, and for the Second forfeit the renewal of his Licence.

That this regulation of the Trade, so far as it relates to the Visitations, the fixing Rates for Goods, and to the delivering Scales & Weights, & Yards, to the Indian Chiefs shall not take place with the Creek Nation (nor with the Chactaw Nation when in Friendship with us) while the French are permitted to hold a Fort in their Country, or until we shall have a Fort among them also by their own Desire. Which Caution will serve to render them uneasy with the French, while they see the Distinction our other Friends enjoy on that account; and dispose them to come into our Measures.

That some of the Chiefs [with a few young Men] of the several Nations of Indians in each District, be encouraged once in the space of 3 or four Years, to pay a Visit at least to the Governours at N. York and Charles Town in So. Carolina respectively; that the Sight of some of the King's Ships [the great number of Merchant Ships,] and vast Plenty and Variety of Goods, according to their usual Effect, may raise great Ideas in them of the British Nation, and of the Importance of our Friendship.

That Provision be made in the Act of Parliament proposed to be passed, for vesting the Direction of the Indian Affairs in his Majesty in manner aforesaid, and for annulling the Acts [or Clauses of Acts] now in force in the several Colonies, that have any Relation to the Indians or their Trade.

1. To prohibit all Persons living in the colonies, to go and Trade in any Indian Nation, without a Licence from one of his Majesty's Commissioners duly obtained. Or to deal with any Indians whatever within the Settlements, other than such as are always resident therein.

2. To prohibit any Goods for the Indian Trade being carried by Land or Sea, and Sold to the French at any of their Settlements or Forts in Canada or Louisiana; or to the Indians of any Nation not in Friendship with us.

3. To declare void all Sales of Lands by the Indians to private Subjects.

4. To empower the Commissioners and Deputies, in a summary way to award small Penalties, or Satisfaction from the Traders to the Indians; to punish Offences of the Rangers; & to apprehend Vagrants and Disorderly Persons, and Criminals, and to send them into the Settlements, to be dealt with according to Law by the respective Governments.

5. To establish a General Provincial Fund, for the Service of all the Colonies with regard to the Indians.

Objects to be kept in view & pursued.

The Objects to be kept in View and pursued under this Plan, besides that of building a Fort or Blockhouse picketted in each Nation of Indians, are

1. The Destruction in general of every French Fort, or House built anywhere in North America upon his Majesty's Lands; to be executed under a proper Military Command from time to time, as a convenient Occasion offers; & as his Majesty shall please to direct.

[52] 2. The Navigation of the Lakes; by securing with very good Forts the fittest Harbours for vessles of Force (after due search,) on the Southside of the Lakes *Ontario & Erie*, and as near as may be *below & above Niagara Fall & Fort between them*. Whereby the French in Canada may be cutt off from any further Communication with the Ohio, & Wabashe, & all the Country to the South of those Lakes, and be confined to the Northside of them. Their Commerce between Montreal & the inland western Settlements being thus doubly liable to be intercepted, may be brought in spite of Niagara Fort at present the Key of the Lakes, tho that Fort were still to stand, to lie at our Mercy; while from the harbour in Lake Erie, our Commerce will be extended through that & the other western Lakes, & vastly encreased with the Indian Nations bordering thereon, whose Dependance on the French, unable to supply them with Goods in the like manner, will consequently be taken off. As that Harbour will lie very convenient to Pensylvania, Maryland, Virginia, & New York (especially if at the East End), the Prospect of Gain will no doubt soon induce People to resort

thither from all those Provinces; who will be a support to it; & probably form a Town. In the meantime a Fort on the Ohio at the most convenient place near its Head, seems absolutely necessary immediately, to intercept the Navigation thereof.

3. The entire Possession of the *Hogohegee*, or great Cherokee River, which intersects from East to West the two Districts of North America above mentioned, so far as its Conflux, together with the Ohio & Wabashe, into the Missisippi. For which purpose, besides the Fort to be built in the Upper Cherokee Towns, there should be one at the Fall towards the midway; & anoth[e]r (by much the strongest & best garrisoned, because in the most important place in No America) at or about the sd Conflux. And by which means, the same forming a Barrier looking both ways, the Communication & mutual Support between Canada & Louisiana, or between New Orleans & Mobile, and the Ohio or Illinois, would be broken. It will be the more secure by its Remoteness from the Chief Strength of both those Provinces. As the whole Country adjacent belongs to our Friends the Cherokees & Chicasaws, who have never suffered the French to take any footing there, tis at present in our power to have an indisputable Right to it. Some of those & other Indians might be induced, by an Annual Present of Ammunition, to settle by the Forts at the Fall & Conflux. Able bodied Men *Convicts* for petty crimes, instead of being hanged, or incorporated among the People of our Colonies, being sent to that distant Fort at the sd Conflux to plant Corn for the use of the Indians, who by their Genius & manner of Living are often reduced to great want of it, will become usefull by attaching them thereby the more to it. And by marrying Indian wives, & having Land allotted to them when their Servitude is expired, they will strengthen the place, & their Offspring prove a valuable sort of Inhabitants. *Trading Houses* being established there, distant Indians before unacquainted with us would soon find the way to them. *Boats* fit for rowing or Sailing, mounting Pattereros,[106] or Blunderbusses,[107] & transporting small Parties of Indians (which would be very agreeable to them) would open the Navigation up & down of the Missisipi & its Streams to the Westward, as well as of the Ohio & Wabashe; and spread Terror every where among our Enemies, the Friends of the French.

---

[106] Pattero, or pedrero—a small cannon or gun used for discharging broken iron, nails, or partridge shot.

[107] A short gun with a large bore and usually a bell muzzle.

[53] 4. The taking Possession at a proper Time of the Mouth of the truly valuable River the *Chattahuchee*, whereon the Lower Creek Nation inhabit; heading near the Lower Cherokee Towns, & one Branch of it near the Upper Creek Towns, & discharging itself through a most fertile Country near the Bay of Apalatchee in the Gulf of Mexico. And for that purpose to keep a strict Watch from the Fort in that Nation, to prevent the French from doing it, who have long had an Eye upon it, the Possession of that River being absolutely necessary to Compleat the Execution of their Scheme, to cut us off from the Indian Nations by a Line of Forts on the back of all our Colonies from the mouth of St. Laurence, *not as is commonly conceived to that of the Missisipi, but of the Chatahuchee*, and would render the Communication between Canada & the Gulf of Mexico vastly shorter. On the other hand it would give us a valuable Port, perhaps fit for large vessles, in that Gulf where we now have none; and furnish us with a water Carriage to the inland Nations, shorter & safer than that of the French. With this view the Bar & Harbour deserve to be surveyed privately, & the River traced to it's Heads. The Hogohegee should be surveyed likewise from its Heads & principal streams in & near the Cherokee Nation, down to its Junction & Conflux with the Ohio & Wabashe into the Missisippi; None of our People having yet gone in Boats upon either of those Rivers.

5. The forming an *Union* among the Indian Nations of the Southern District, who shall come into the Treaty proposed to be made, like that of the Six united Nations of N York; to be maintained by a General Council of the Chiefs of each Nation, to make Peace or War with other Nations by joint Consent, to adjust amicably any Mischeif or Differences arising between the People of one Nation with those of another, and to consult upon whatever concerns their general or particular Welfare. Which Union is practicable to be effected, by a judicious use & application of their different Circumstances, Situations, Characters & Dispositions; linking *by the Steps that maybe taken* one Nation after another to the Cherokees, (who hold the most important Country) as having made the first Treaty in England with his Majesty; and to whom therefore the Envoy ought to apply first to make the new Treaty now proposed. This Union would produce every happy consequence that can be wished for. It would confirm & strengthen the Six Nations now wavering, or rather inclining to desert us; Or if they should, unfortunately

for us, go over altogether to the French; it would strike a Terror into them, & either regain them, or put a stop to the terrible Calamities which must otherways befall all our Colonies in general. And even tho the Creeks, as well as the Chactaws, should not be easily or soon, or not at all brought into this Union, yet the Cherokees, Catawbas, & Chicasaws (who undoubtedly may be brought into it) being properly disposed & supported from [one] End to the other of the Hogohegee, (as they might be supported without our being obliged to go through the Creek or any other Indian Country) would be sufficient to render abortive the French plan, being by themselves a formidable Alliance, & an over match for all the other Indians either on the Northside or the Southside of that Central River which divides the whole. Therefore they would become the Umpires or Arbitrators, among the Indians on both sides.

[54] The Provincial Fund for that Part of the Expence to be defrayed by the several Colonies, may be established in the most equal manner[.]

Provincial Funds
for that part of
the Expence to
be defrayed by
the Colonies.

1st. By a Poll-Tax, payable annually by every British male subject therein; which at a very Moderate Rate, will Raise a Sum sufficient for other purposes besides. And by means thereof the strength of each Province will be always known. Or if this Tax is not thought advisable to be imposed by the Parliament; then

2. By a small Duty on Wines imported from Madeira, the Western Islands, & the Canaries, and on Sugar, Melasses, & Rum from our [own] Islands; and..........................
also an easy Duty on *forreign* Sugars, Melasses & Rum imported in Brit[*t*]ish Bottoms, instead of that now payable; which last alone (being indeed the most eligible) would bring in a considerable Sum more than sufficient for this purpose. Whereas the present Duties thereon being very high, & the Temptation to smuggling it consequently very great, a very small sum arises thereon to the Crown in all the Colonies, far from sufficient to pay the Charge of collecting. And what is worse, immense Quantities of those articles are brought in French Bottoms at least as far as Cape Breton, which is made a kind of Free Port, from whence as at next door they are easily run into our Northern Settlements, as well by their as our own vessles, in Exchange for Fish, Lumber, &c for their Sugar Islands; to the great encrease of the French Navigation, & their Manufacture of Rum, which they are encouraged to employ many hands in making for our use,

not using it themselves. As to what regards our own Sugar Islands in this respect, it is evident, that it would be a vast national Advantage to Great Britain, inasmuch as it would greatly encrease it's Navigation & National Profit many ways, if the whole Crop of the French Sugar Islands could possibly be imported into our own Colonies in British Bottoms. All above their own Consumption, would be reshipped to Great Britain & Ireland in the like Bottoms, in payment for Manufactures. And all beyond the Consumption here, would be again reshipped in the like manner to the other Markets in Europe, with the certain Gain of three Freights, Commissions & other Charges. And as the Market price here of the French as well as English Sugar would necessarily be governed in that case by the general Market price of Europe, there could no Hardship arise to the Planters of our own Sugar Islands; who would obtain the true value of their Produce, tho' not so much more than it's value at any other Market in Europe as at present, when not making enough for our Consumption they have their own price for them. The Duties collected in No America upon forreign Sugars, Melasses & Rum &ca (Merchandize & Prize) ever since the year 1733, having not been appropriated by that Act to any particular use, remain I apprehend still in hand to be applied; amounting to a pretty good sum.

3. By Post offices established, for the conveyance of Letters, throughout North America; which are much wanted, & would under good Regulations bring in a large sum.

[55] The Tax or Duties aforesaid to be granted to his Majesty, & appropriated to the Securing the British Interest & the Commerce of the Colonies in general with the Indian Nations in North America. The same to be brought together into one Treasury in each District, to wit at New York & at South Carolina; and to be issued for the said Service by his Majesty's warrant, or by the warrant or Certificate of the Commissioner General in each district, pursuant to his Majesty's Instructions, & with the advice of the Provincial Deputies. A Deficiency in either Treasury at any time to be supplied out of the other. And the accounts to be subject to be examined by the Council & Assembly in the respective Colonies, for the entire Satisfaction of all his Majesty's Subjects therein; which accounts will of course be audited by the Auditor General of his Majesty's Revenues in America.

I have now, my Lords, finished what I proposed to offer concerning the Indian Affairs in North America. It will not be admired, if in what relates to the Northern District I have been less particular, or appeared less correct, than in what relates to the Southern one; having not been alike intimately acquainted with every circumstance in the former as in the latter. And whatever Defects or Imperfections may appear, in the Plan for retreiving & establishing our Interest among all the Indian Nations in both Districts, they will easily be corrected by your Lordship's own Penetration & Judgment. Upon the whole I flatter myself, that it will be found on due Consideration, sufficient (the case of the present Invasion of our Colony Territories excepted) to answer fully for the future the End proposed with respect to the Indians, by an Union or association among our Colonies on the Continent, so much talked of & wished for in general of late: but scarce practicable (anymore than a general Regulation of the Indian Trade is among themselves) as being highly improbable to be jointly agreed on by all, in regard both to the Measures & the Expence; Or if with great Pains to be effected, yet subject to such clogs as would often render it in a manner fruitless, & indeed always insufficient to produce the Effects proposed by this Plan. Besides that an Union or Association of any kind between dependent Colonies, doth not seem to be consistent with the true Policy of any Mother Country. This Plan is simple & plain, not dependent on various Deliberations, or subject to Accidents. The measures to be executed, are to flow from the proper Fountain his Majesty, cloathed with full Authority & Power in himself, & his hands strengthened with money.

I am with all due Respect
My Lords
Your Lordships most obedient
& devoted Servant
[(Signed) EDMD ATKIN]

INDEX

Index

Abeka (Creek town), 64 and n.

Abeka Indians (Creeks): population and location of, 43

Abihka; *see* Abeka

Adair, James: criticisms of Atkin, xvii, xviii n.; in Chotaw revolt, xxi n.; compared with Atkin as a writer, xxxii-xxxiii; on fellow-traders, 8 n.; on French priests, 13 n.

Adair's History: map of, frontispiece, 74 and n.; discussion of, xxxii-xxxiii

Agan, Florence, 69

Agencies in Indian management, refusal of, 28 and n.; *see also* South Carolina

Aix-la-Chapelle, Treaty of, xv

Alabama Fort; *see* Fort Toulouse

Alabama Garrison; *see* Fort Toulouse

Alabama Indians (Albahamas, Alibamaes, Creeks), xvii, 5, 43, 59-60

Alabama River, 58

Albany, N.Y., 15, 16; conference at in 1754, xxxv

Alden, Professor John R., xvii, xxxv

Allegheny (Aligany) River, 5

Altamaha River, 57, 74

Ammunition, 10, 73, 83; low cost of, 11; expense in carriage of, 11; French supply Indians with, 12; for war and hunting, 22-23; lack of, in Louisiana, 23; for Creeks, 58; powder and ball, 86; annual present of, 91; *see also* Indian presents; Indian trade and traders

Andrews, Thomas, 30 n.

Apalachee Bay, 5, 54, 92

Apalachee Indians, 57; defeat of, 56 and n., 63; woman wife of Peter Chartier, 66

Apalachicola Indians (Creeks), 57

Apalachicola River, 54; country of, 55

Appalachian Mountains, xxxi; British confined to, xvi; as sources of rivers, 48

Arkansas River, 68

Assemblies; *see* Colonial Assemblies; South Carolina Assembly

Atkin, Edmond: writings of, vii, xx n., xxx ff.; appointed superintendent, xvi, xxii; death of, xvi, xxix; importance of work of, xvi ff.; xxix ff.; personality of, attacked by warrior, xvii; expenses of, xvii, xxviii; aids Washington and Forbes, xvii, xxiii; speech of, to Choctaw, xviii; early life of, xviii; business activities and land of, xviii and n.; will of, xviii n.; appointed to Council, xviii, 3; interest in Indian affairs, xviii-xix; opposes Assembly, xix; defends

royal interests, xix; dispute of, with Rutledge, xix; opinion of South Carolina government, xx; travels of, xx ff.; relations with Loudoun, xxii; salary of, xxii n; assisted by Gist, xxiii; opposes scalp bounties, xxiv, xxvii; work of, on Virginia frontier, xxv; seal of office of, xxv n.; assisted by Byrd, xxvi; work in South Sarolina and in Creek and Choctaw country, xxvii; health of, xxviii and n.; marriage of, xxviii-xxix; accomplishments of, xxix, xxxv-xxxvi; offices of, xxix n.; Indian presents ordered by, xxx; on French Indian policy, xxxi ff.; report of, xxxi ff., 1 ff., facing p. 2; on Indian traders, xxxii; on Indian virtues, xxxii; plan of, xxxiii ff., 77 ff.; requested to write on Indian affairs, 3; views on mercantile system, 93-94

Atkin, John, xviii and n.

Atkin, Lady Anne, xxix n.

Atkins, business firm of, xxxv n.

Atlantic Ocean, river mouths on, 4

Attakullakulla (Little Carpenter, Cherokee chief): friend of English, xxviii; rescues John Stuart, xxviii; visits London, xxviii n.; suspected of French sympathies, 5 n.

Augusta, Ga., 34, 74

Augusta rum trade, 35, 62

Autossity Ustonecka (Outacite, Cherokee chief), 50 and n., facing p. 50

Baskets of Cherokee, 49

Beasts of prey, destroyed by Indians, 45

Bedford, Duke of, 31 n., 33

Bellin, Jacques Nicolas, maps of, 61and n.

Bienville, Jean Baptiste Lemoyne, Sieur de, 55 n.

Black Warrior River, 74 n.

Blacksmiths for Indians, xxx n.; *see also* Gunsmiths

Blankets for Indians, xxx

Blockhouses, 78, 79 ff., 90

Blunderbusses, mounted on boats, 91

Board of Trade, xvi, xviii, xx, xxii, xxvi, xxx, xxxi, xxxv, 77, 82, 84; functions and powers of, 1 and n.

Boats: for Indian trade, 88; proposed uses of, 91; not used by British on inland rivers, 92; *see also* Ships

Bosomworth, Abraham, 20 n., 33 n.

Boston, xxii; fur trade of, 16

Bounties for scalps, xxiv; *see also* Scalping

Braddock, Major General Edward, xvi, xxii n.

99

—INDEX—

Edmond; Johnson, William; Rogers, Robert; Stuart, John

Indian towns, xxxiii, 6 n., 25, 27; *see also* towns under tribal names

Indian trade (fur and skin trade), xix, xxi, xxix and n., xxxi; abuses in, xxxiv, 23; commissioner for, 18; in Georgia, 33 ff.; French, xxxiv and n., 7, 71 ff.; Anglo-French rivalry in, 6, 7-13, 24; intercolonial rivalry for Indians, 22 and n., 23, 25; beads of, facing p. 24; paths, facing p. 34; importance of, 36; need of regulation for, 40; with Chickasaw, 69; weights and scales for, xxxiv, 85-86; *see also* French; Indian traders; Indian treaties

Indian trade, regulations and laws for, xxxiv, 13; to be repealed, 77; proposed, 85 ff.; in New York, 15; in South Carolina, xxxiii n., 17, 21 and n., 24 ff., 27 ff.

Indian traders, xv, 6, 37, 45-46, 69; oppose Atkin, xxviii; French, xxxi; undesirable characteristics of, xxxii, 8, 22; extent of territory covered, 11-12; in Pennsylvania, 14; rivalry in New York, 16; licenses of, 18 ff., 34, 79, 86; journals of, 22; influence of, 23; reside in Indian towns, 25; responsibilities and obligations of, 29, 78, 87 ff.; as interpreters, 29 and n.; equipment of, 34; undersell each other, 35; private interests of, 39; in Natchez war, 39; among Cherokee, 52; early history of, 59; killed by French, 72; boldness of, 73

Indian treaties, xxxii, xxxiv; in New York, 14; Indian observance of, 38; to be negotiated by British government, 41; with Choctaw, 72, 73; proposed, 77 ff., 92; obligations of Indians under, 78 ff.

Indian wars: warriors in, xxiv, xxv, 4; causes of, 23, 38; *see also* Ammunition; French; Indian treaties; Indian weapons; Indian trade and traders; Indian tribal names

Indian weapons: guns, 9-10, 81; cutlass, 35; hatchets, 81

Indian women: plant maize, xv; warlike conduct of, 68; as wives of soldiers, 80; as wives of convicts, 91

Indians: longevity of, xv; appearance of, xv, 68; importance of, xxi, 3; character of, xxxii, 10, 38 ff.; not dominated by forts, 9; ideas of equity and value, 39; *see also* classifications under Indian and tribal names

Indians and liquor; *see* Drunkenness; Liquor; Rum

Iroquois (Six Nations), xxix, xxxi, xxxiv, 4, 13, 14, 36, 41, 77, 84, 92; in part join Montcalm, xvi; influenced by William Johnson, xvi n.; policy of neutrality, 7; tribes of, listed, 14 n.; in fur trade, 15; living at Montreal, 23; population of, 41; losses against Catawba, 51 n.; related to Nottaway, 51 n.; alliance with Cherokee, 52; *see also* Caughnawaga; Cayuga; Oneida; Mohawk; Onondaga; Seneca; Tuscarora

Jamaica, 56

Jesuits, xv and n.

Johnson, Sir William, xvii, xxii, xxix, xxx and n., xxxv, 15 n.; appointed superintendent, xvi; keeps Iroquois neutral, xvi and n.; on scalping, xxiv; on liquor for Indians, 27 n.

Jumonville, Joseph Coulon de Villiers, Sieur de, xvi

Kennedy, Archibald, xxxv

Keowee (Cherokee town), xxvi, 48, 52, 85; trail to, 53 n.; fort near, 54

Keowee River, 54

King George's War, 23

King Hagler (Catawba chief), on liquor, 27 n.

Knives for Indians, 10

Lake Erie, 4, 15, 61, 70, 90

Lake Ontario, 14, 15, 90; French navigation on, 36

Lampriere, Capt., 57

Lancaster, Pa., 14 and n.

Land; *see* Indian lands

LaSalle, Robert Cavelier Sieur de, 65 n.; anecdotes relating to, 59

Laws; *see* Indian trade, regulations and laws for; Indian traders; Scalping; Taxes

Leather, 25, 85; *see also* Indian trade; Indian traders

Lewis, Maj. Andrew, xxviii n.

Licenses for traders; *see* Indian traders

Limnate, 4

Liquor, 14, 59, 62, 83, 87; diluted with water, xxxiv, 88; destroys Indians, 26; King Hagler's opinion of, 27 n.; proposed duties on, 93; *see also* Drunkenness; Punch; Rum

Little Tennessee River, xxviii n.

Loire, Sieur de, 59

London, England, xx

Loudoun, Earl of; *see* Campbell, John